the Paddling Chef

A Cookbook for Canoeists, Kayakers, and Rafters

the Paddling Chef

A Cookbook for Canoeists, Kayakers, and Rafters

Dian Weimer
Second Edition

FOX CHAPEL
PUBLISHING

© 2012 by Fox Chapel Publishing Company, Inc., East Petersburg, PA.

The Paddling Chef is an original work, first published in Canada in 2008 by The Heliconia Press, under the title *The Paddling Chef* and ISBN 978-1-896980-44-7. *The Paddling Chef, Second Edition* was first published in North America in 2012 by Fox Chapel Publishing Company. All rights reserved.

ISBN 978-1-56523-714-8

Library of Congress Cataloging-in-Publication Data

Weimer, Dian, 1948-
The paddling chef : a cookbook for canoeists, kayakers, and rafters / Dian Weimer. -- 2nd ed.
    p. cm.
Includes index.
ISBN 978-1-56523-714-8 (pbk.)
1. Outdoor cooking. I. Title.
TX823W443 2012
641.5'78--dc23
                        2011047866

5036 3901 11/12

· To learn more about the other great books from Fox Chapel Publishing, or to find a retailer near you, call toll-free 800-457-9112 or visit us at *www.FoxChapelPublishing.com*.

Note to Authors: We are always looking for talented authors to write new books. Please send a brief letter describing your idea to Acquisition Editor, 1970 Broad Street, East Petersburg, PA 17520.

Printed in the United States of America
First printing

This book is dedicated
to my late father,
who inspired my love of the sea.

Contents

Many thanks to some special people who have encouraged and supported me in my paddling adventures and to write this book.

To Leslie Churchland, my paddling partner, for her steadfast friendship and enthusiasm for our continuing paddling adventures together.

To Michael LeGeyt and Don Knight, Rodney Allan Badger and Martine Reid, special friends and avid canoeists, with whom I have been fortunate to have shared paddling trips and some wonderful meals.

To my son, Erik, my companion on my first experience in a kayak.

To my daughter, Lindsay, who has been a most delightful paddling companion, sharing her youthful enthusiasm and her love of poetry and song.

To my husband, Jim, who has not the slightest interest in either paddling or camping, but who is most supportive of my adventures and keeps the home fires burning.

PREFACE

Having been born and raised in Vancouver, a jewel of a city on the Pacific coast, I've always had a love of the sea. But I was unprepared for the passion that has become part of my middle-aged life – adventure trips paddling in a kayak.

My family was invited to spend a weekend with my great friend Leslie Churchland and her family at their summer home on Bowen Island. Leslie suggested that we take our two older children, then twelve, for a kayak lesson at the recently opened kayak rental shop at Mt. Gardner Bay. The proprietor was an amiable, gentle-spirited young man. He inspired us with his passion for the sea and its inhabitants, flora and fauna, and taught us how to trust the kayaks by having us stand up in the boats, playing a racing game. We were hooked!

Over the years, the West coast of British Columbia has enticed us to expand our horizons on ever-more challenging paddling adventures. Over time, Leslie has taken charge of charts and tide tables, while I've become the chef and meal planner. This division of labor has worked well for us.

The first few multi-day trips were undertaken with our young daughters, but as we expanded our horizons from the Howe Sound region, subsequent trips have been taken on our own.

From the beginning, the quality of our meals has been an important consideration. There is nothing more satisfying than enjoying a good meal, accompanied by a glass of wine, at the end of a long day's paddle. On a dreary, drizzly day or in retreat under the tarp in a downpour, a hearty soup or bowl of chili is most satisfying.

Nothing diminishes a trip more than poorly planned or prepared meals. After personal safety and comfort, the quality and quantity of food can make or break a trip. Gorp and power bars are reserved for those days when getting an early start is essential, or when lunch is eaten on the water.

As I've taken trips in a kayak with friends who are canoeists, (on lakes, rivers and the ocean), and rafters. I have written this book for all species of paddler. Kayaks, canoes and river rafts can accommodate many pounds of food. The intent of this book is to provide practical, tasty recipes and some more ambitious meal ideas for adventurous chefs. Almost all of the recipes can easily be multiplied for additional servings. Most of the recipes have options for variations according to your own taste and most can be adapted to serve later in a trip.

Ours is a multicultural society and we have the opportunity to enjoy cuisines from all over the world. I've included a sampling of some possibilities throughout this book.

Longer trips provide a challenge for those of us reluctant to resort to a package of dried pasta on the last night of a two-week trip. I've made suggestions for drying food that can be rehydrated, so that meals can still have variety and fresh flavors late in a trip. I have also given consideration to waste. After paddling for two weeks in Gwaii Haanas Park (Queen Charlotte Islands, B.C.), Leslie and I had only a small plastic garbage bag containing, for the most part, onion and garlic skins and other bits of vegetable waste, vacuum tuna and salmon packets, some tin foil refuse and an empty ham tin. Our empty ziplock bags remained in a dry bag to be used on another adventure.

Burning is not often an option in the summer, as campfires are banned in many areas due to the risk of forest fires. In my years of paddling, I've only had two opportunities to make a summer campfire. Fires were allowed in Gwaii Haanas Park, but there wasn't much driftwood available on the beaches. This is damp moss, not dry driftwood, territory. I managed a tiny fire one evening, although I must confess, campfires are not a priority for Leslie and me. However, on my Bowron Lakes trip with Michael and Don, as the temperature dropped, we would have loved to make a cozy fire. The ban was lifted only on our last night, after much rain had fallen.

Because the paddling chef has to carry enough fuel for the duration of the trip, I've made fuel conservation a consideration; almost all the recipes require less than half an hour on the stove.

I have shared excerpts from my journals and anecdotes of culinary successes as well as some notable failures. Landing on a beach at a perfect campsite on a warm summer's day inspires the paddling chef to prepare a carefully crafted meal. But landing in the rain, having to pitch the tent, raise the tarp and prepare something to quell the rumblings of a hungry stomach is a challenge. Any chef will tell you that all does not go well in the kitchen every day, whether that kitchen is in a five-star hotel dining room or on a log on a beach.

Pre-packaged 'camp' food is expensive and, frankly, rather boring. Hikers and mountaineers are much more limited by weight considerations, as they have to pack all their gear, including food, in their backpacks. Paddlers can explore a wide range of possibilities. Lots of fresh foods will travel well. With a little thought and some time preparing menus at home, happy eating on a canoe, rafting or kayak trip can be as much a part of the adventure as the destination.

– Dian Weimer

Symbols Used for the Recipes

Degree of Difficulty

Easy—the recipe calls for only a few ingredients and timing is straightforward.

Moderate—the recipe requires more than one process (e.g., the making of a sauce), so timing is more of an issue.

Complex—the recipe requires the help of more than one paddling chef and some basic cooking skills are required.

 Number of Pots or Pans

The reference for pots or pans is only for the recipe. If you are serving rice or a vegetable, you will need an additional burner if you're using pocket burners that clamp onto the fuel tank and not a Coleman type stove. Recipes for salads, sauces or dressings that can be mixed in a small bowl, not requiring a burner, will have no pot.

Timing

15 min: the recipe should take 15 minutes or less to prepare and serve

30 min: the recipe should take 30 minutes or less to serve and may include preparation time such as marinating

60 min: the recipe likely includes several steps including marinating or sauce preparation before serving

 Vegetarian

People define themselves as "vegetarian" in several ways. Some don't eat meat, but will eat fish or eggs and cheese. Others won't eat any products that come from an animal that can look you in the eye. Vegans will neither eat nor wear any product that comes from an animal.

My vegetarian recipes exclude dishes containing butter, eggs, meat or cheese that are important for the success of the recipe. But if tofu can be easily substituted for the meat or if other vegetables can be added, olive oil substituted for the butter and the cheese eliminated—or if the recipe is already vegetarian—you will find a leaf beside the recipe.

The Chef's Dilemma

MENU PLANNING

Planning the food for a paddling trip can be great fun but it can also be time consuming and problematic if the chef doesn't know where to start. Begin with foods that you and your paddling companions like to eat. Make sure that no one in the group has any food allergies before planning your menus. After all, you're on a holiday and should enjoy your well-earned vacation to the fullest. Then ask yourself some pertinent questions.

How long is the trip?

What fresh foods can be taken? If the trip is longer than a week, considerations need to be made for taking dried, freeze-dried, canned or pre-packaged food, as most fresh foods won't last longer than seven days. Despite everyone's best efforts, fresh foods tend to get bumped and bruised, especially when being packed and unpacked in and out of dry bags. Canoeists and rafters have the option of transporting a cooler or larger plastic containers, which serve well for protecting food.

How many are in the party?

For a solo paddler or a pair, some foods just don't make any sense. A tinned ham, for example, can't be consumed in one meal unless, perhaps, you are two extremely hungry men! You'll end up with fresh meat leftovers that must either be disposed of or eaten the next day. However, if you really like ham, as Leslie and I do, it will provide a tasty dinner and meat for the following day's breakfast or lunch, late in a trip.

It's easy to find recipes to prepare for a group of four to six. Larger groups, of course, require more burners and chefs or consideration for simple recipes that can be made in a large batch. In camp at Little Kaikash, on our trip to Johnstone Strait, we observed two very hardworking, young female guides preparing breakfast quesadillas for their thirteen paddling guests.

What is the preparation time for the meal?

Meals prepared at camp on a weekend trip, or on a leisurely summer's evening entail different considerations than those made after landing late on a stormy day. Plan for flexibility when brainstorming meal ideas. Have additional foods on hand for all kinds of weather and potential delays in the trip plan. These are usually easy-to-prepare items such as pre-packaged soups and sauces, pasta, vacuum packed tuna, salmon and the like. As I've said, most of the recipes in this book consider time and fuel conservation: I don't often care to spend more than half an hour over dinner preparations.

Bowron Lakes
1975, Rodney Allan Badger

On my first long trip, the Bowron Lakes, with several miles of portages, I counted crackers and cookies, weighed portions carefully, and trusted the packages or recipes when they said "Serves 4". As a result, one large man on the crew complained of short rations and of being hungry.

When planning the next trip, I offered nuts or a cup of instant soup while I cooked the main meal. I also provided small zip lock bags for everyone to fill from a common bag of gorp, nuts, jerky and candy in the morning, so they could nibble all day.

Isaac Lake

Bowron Lakes 2008

dw

Do you want to transport canned foods?
If "yes", what's your weight limit?

Canoes and rafts can accommodate large amounts of food, but weight can be an important issue on a trip that entails portages. Also, carrying empty cans in the garbage bag, even crushed ones, can be a nuisance, if not a weighty one, for all paddlers. But some canned food is often an important component of a paddler's food stores, especially on a longer trip.

Are you going to fish?
What if you don't catch anything?

Time is the major consideration if you plan to fish, although trolling while paddling is also possible. You need quite a leisurely day on the water, as normal paddling speed is too fast for most trolled lures. What is your traveling agenda? Do you have two or three days at one campsite where you can spend a relaxed afternoon fishing? Everyone in the group needs to agree to take time for fishing.

Leslie and I spent three days in camp at Big Bunsby Island, north of Kyuquot, and had plans to fish one day. Unfortunately, Mother Nature had other ideas and we found ourselves hunkered down with blowing southeasterly gale force winds and teeming rain battering our tent. The best laid plans...

Are you in bear country?

On my trip with Michael and Don to the Bowron Lakes, we decided not to take bacon because of its strong aroma and bears' superb sense of smell. However, we found ourselves one day sharing a campsite with three experienced outdoorsmen from Alberta and were positively salivating when they made fried eggs and bacon for breakfast. Some parks in areas frequented by bears have metal bear-proof containers to store food. Bowron Lakes Provincial Park is one of these. Just be aware of what you're doing and clean up well.

Leslie and I try to camp on islands, if possible, but this is no guarantee that you won't be visited by a bear. They are excellent swimmers. Generally speaking, they're not interested in people. Canoeists and rafters are somewhat more likely than kayakers to encounter bears, as you are most often traveling in inland regions and mountain territory. This is particularly true of grizzlies. That being said, some black bears and grizzlies have found the seashore to be an abundant source of food. We discovered fresh bear dung near our last camp on Tanu Island in Gwaii Haanas Park, and a big black bear was occupying the beach we were heading for on the Acous Peninsula, on Vancouver Island. We startled a young bear while paddling Okeover Inlet on our Desolation Sound trip and sent him scrambling up the hillside. A handsome black bear we spotted only fifty feet away from our camp at Cable Beach, in Clayoquot Sound took no interest in us and wandered down the beach to disappear into the woods. Although you might need to access it as a water source, don't camp close to a stream feeding into a lake or the ocean. Both grizzlies and black bears can be found near streams, especially during spawning season. Caution and common sense is the key.

The bottom line is to keep a very clean camp. Never take food into your tent or sleep in clothes that you've worn while preparing a meal. Hang your food as high and as well away from your campsite as you can. Most self-respecting bears can get at your food if they're determined to do so. But mice and raccoons are also often about, so do hang your food if at all possible. An acquaintance of mine who has done some paddling told me of an experience he had with a raccoon while camped on an island in Desolation Sound. He and his paddling partner had stowed their food in a back hatch. When they were awakened during the night by a sound near their kayaks, they attributed it to a seal. In the morning, much to their astonishment, they discovered the hatch cover slipped aside but still latched down, the neoprene cover ripped and food scattered about. The vacuum package of cheese had been chomped on and candy wrappers, strewn along the beach, formed a little path to the woods. When they were preparing breakfast with the food that could be salvaged, the little thief reappeared to see what was being served. This illustrates another imperative – never stow food in your canoe or kayak. While a raccoon will just ruin your meal choices, a bear could destroy your boat, leaving you without your means of transportation.

Put it together

Sit down and answer the questions posed earlier in this chapter. Some foods will fall by the wayside and others will appear to be wise choices for preparing flavorful meals in camp.

Write down recipes and food ideas on recipe cards, or put them in a file in your computer. If you've used recipe cards, sit down at a table and arrange them in a grid; breakfast, lunch and dinner for the number of days of your trip. If you've used your computer, do the same with a spreadsheet. Both are handy ways to see how your meals will unfold. If you really want to go over the top about food planning, there are software programs available; enter a recipe and the program will multiply the ingredients for the recipe by the number of servings and generate a shopping list.

After a trip, refer back to your spreadsheet and comment on the successes, ideas for variations and the recipes that didn't work for you. Over time, you'll have a great list of favorite recipes and will have compiled an efficient list of foods to pack—although the keen chef will always be looking for challenging new recipes to raise the bar for culinary experiences on a paddling trip.

Kyuquot, Bunsby Islands

Taking the ferry from Horseshoe Bay to Nanaimo, we drove to Gold River on a hot summer's day. After an overnight stay in Gold River, we loaded our kayak and all our gear on the MV Uchuck III early the following morning. We spent eleven hours on board the Uchuck, stopping to unload supplies to the log sort camps, fish farms and fishing lodges along the way. Two other paddling groups with both canoes and kayaks were on board. Most of the other passengers taking the overnight trip to Kyuquot were older couples who love the sea but just can't manage their own boats anymore.

Unfortunately, the fine summer weather deteriorated during the day. We finally landed at Kyuquot at eight o'clock in the evening. Two burly men picked up our big, loaded kayak, and placed it on a pallet; Leslie and I climbed into our respective cockpits. The crane swung us over the side, placed us gently onto the water, and we paddled to shore.

Rain drizzled down. We asked if we could pay to join the others, who were staying overnight, for dinner. We were granted this luxury, seated outside the restaurant on a little covered patio, and had a wonderful meal of salmon, pasta and salads. They weren't disparaging of us; they simply didn't have room in the restaurant for two extra guests! We were relieved at not having to prepare a meal in the rain at nine o'clock.

We camped that night in the front yard of an old, run-down cabin. The owner, Tom, was away and we were told he wouldn't mind us camping in the charming old garden in front of his home. We rose to a fine morning. A Rufous Hummingbird flitted around the perennial fuschias as the sun came up.

Following is the list of food and meals we prepared for our week-long paddle to the Bunsby Islands out of Kyuquot, on the west coast of Vancouver Island. It is fairly basic, but can easily be expanded to include fresh meats, herbs and spices to make more exotic dishes or dried food for a longer trip. Although we could have transported frozen meat in a cooler to Gold River, we were two days from our first camp dinner, so we chose not to take fresh meat on this trip.

A Sample Shopping List

for a week-long trip with 2 people

(Used for our Kyuquot, Bunsby Islands trip)

FRESH	
English cucumber	1
Green peppers	2
Salad greens	large (27cm x 28 cm) zip lock bag
Cherry tomatoes	small plastic container
LONGER LASTING	
Eggs	1 dozen
Apples	4 apples
Oranges	4 oranges
Butter	a half-pound, in plastic container
Onions, garlic	several small onions, garlic
Commercial container of lemon juice	
Carrots	package of peeled carrots
Cheddar cheese	a half-pound, in several foil-wrapped pieces
Havarti cheese	a half-pound, in several foil-wrapped pieces
Grated Parmesan cheese	small container
Feta cheese	small container
Camembert cheese rounds	4
Salami sausage	1
Pepperoni	several long sticks
English muffins	package of 6
Pita bread	package of 6
Salad dressing	small bottle

LONGEST LASTING

Tuna, salmon	2 vacuum packages of tuna, 1 salmon
Dried bacon	2 sealed packages, 6 slices in each
Tinned ham	1 for the last two days
Dried pasta: rotini	zip lock bag
Dried pastas with sauce	4 packages
Dried chili	1 cup
Rice	3 packages
Bisquick mix—crêpes and pancakes	zip lock bags
Spaghetti sauce	small can
Dried soups	4 packages
Packaged sauces (pesto, carbonara, mushroom)	1 each
Dried wild mushrooms	zip lock bag
Dry milk powder	zip lock bag
Chicken bouillon cubes	several in a zip lock bag
Sturdy crackers: Stoned Wheat Thins	in plastic container
Oatmeal in individual packages	12
Trail mix, power bars	
Cookies	plastic container
Coffee	1 pound in a plastic container
Olive oil, maple syrup	small bottle of each
Wine, port, cider, 6 V8 juice boxes	
Salt, pepper, rosemary, oregano, red pepper flakes	

A Sample Menu

for a week-long trip with 2 people

JULY 16

Departing from overnight camp at Kyuquot after retrieving gear from the
MV Uchuck III

BREAKFAST:	hot oatmeal, one half an orange each, coffee
LUNCH:	soup, Cheddar cheese, pita bread, salami, salad
PRE-DINNER:	Camembert cheese with crackers
DINNER:	rotini with tuna, reconstituted wild mushrooms, green peppers, carbonara sauce and salad

JULY 17

At camp in the Bunsby Islands

BREAKFAST:	V8 juice, poached eggs on an English muffin, bacon, coffee
LUNCH:	al fresco on a day trip—pepperoni sticks, Cheddar cheese, pita bread, carrots, cucumber slices, cherry tomatoes
DINNER:	chili with pepperoni chunks and Greek salad

JULY 18

BREAKFAST:	one half an orange each, pancakes with bacon, coffee
LUNCH:	al fresco on a day trip—salami, Havarti cheese, pita bread, cucumber slices, carrots, apple
PRE-DINNER:	Camembert cheese with crackers
DINNER:	salmon with sautéed slices of green pepper, onion, lemon sauce, served over rice. Salad. Half an apple each for dessert

JULY 19

Gale force winds and teeming rain—stayed in the tent until noon—meals prepared during the storm in the lee under the protection of a stand of trees.
No tarp—it was protecting the tent!

BREAKFAST/ LUNCH:	cream of asparagus soup, salami slices (me) oatmeal and coffee (Leslie)
PRE-DINNER:	Camembert cheese with crackers
DINNER:	pasta with pesto sauce, tuna and Parmesan (We actually had a lively conversation at dinner!)

JULY 20

BREAKFAST:	V8 juice, bacon and eggs, English muffins, coffee
LUNCH:	soup, salami, pita bread, Havarti cheese, carrots, cucumber slices, cherry tomatoes
DINNER:	rotini with spaghetti sauce, chopped pepperoni, Parmesan. Half an apple each for dessert

JULY 21

6:30 a.m. departure from the Bunsby Islands to Spring Island

BREAKFAST:	hot oatmeal, one half an orange each
SPRING ISLAND	
LUNCH:	grilled ham and Cheddar on an English muffin, cherry tomatoes
DINNER:	frittata with onions, green pepper, Parmesan, fresh chanterelles, diced pepperoni

JULY 22

BREAKFAST:	poached eggs on an English muffin, bacon, one half an orange each, coffee
LUNCH:	Cheddar cheese with crackers, cucumber slices, pepperoni, salami
PRE-DINNER:	Camembert cheese with crackers
DINNER:	ham with sautéed sliced apples, rice, glazed carrots

JULY 23

6:30 a.m. departure to Kyuquot

BREAKFAST:	V8 Juice, hot oatmeal

The Chef's Second Dilemma
KEEPING
ORGANIZED

Where's the Garlic?

One of the frustrations in dealing with food on my kayak trips over the years has been in knowing where to find things in dry bags. Life is much easier for canoeists and rafters if you transport food in a plastic bin or cooler. This became evident to me when I was paddling the Bowron Lakes with my longtime friends, Michael and Don. Michael carried his food in a large, rectangular, insulated bag and when he unzipped the large top, it was pretty easy for him to find what he was looking for. We shared a campsite another night with three men who carried their food in a large plastic bin.

Canoeists and rafters using dry bags, as some do especially when traveling in bear country, will suffer the same frustrations as kayakers. You can't hang a plastic tub from a tree! While a dry bag is great to stuff in a hatch or a cockpit, or lash under the thwart, digging down to the bottom of one to retrieve an onion or package of cheese and then having to repack the bag is not only annoying, it's one of the main reasons that foods get banged up and damaged, thus shortening their traveling life.

I've tried several methods of packing and still have some frustrations, but here are a few suggestions to help you to remember where you've stored things. I have variously organized food by meals, by fresh, longer lasting, longest lasting and by food types. So far I have come up with a hybrid of these three; the method that works best for me. You will probably have to take several trips and experiment to find what method of organization works best for you. The duration of the trip is also a factor. Certainly, if you're taking a tinned ham that you have no intention of eating until the last day, put it in the bottom of a bag and forget about it. Besides, it's heavy. You don't want it squashing or damaging other foods. But then you will encounter some of the ingredients you pack to accompany this last dinner along the way and will have to dig through a repacked bag. Therein lies the frustration.

Rodney Badger, a seasoned canoeist and river rafter who plans the meals for many of his extensive trips, uses the 'meal' organization method. He takes dry bags on his canoe or rafting trips labeled "Breakfast", "Lunch", and "Dinner" and has a fourth bag for condiments. He even labels his meals "L1", "D2", and so forth. But he also most often travels with a larger group than I do. So, the size of the group is also a consideration when organizing the food stores. The paddling chef should be in charge even if others are enlisted to help with meal preparations.

If you are taking spices or other small amounts of ingredients that you will use for only one recipe, combine them at home and put them into the plastic container from a 35 mm roll of film or a similar small container. This also works for liquids such as red wine or balsamic vinegar, if they're also only being taken to make one recipe. Make sure that you pack the little container in a zip lock bag with the other ingredients to make the recipe; otherwise you'll never find it!

Some of these suggestions may seem obvious, but bear mentioning.

1. Take dry bags of different colors and label them.

2. Pack your frozen meat in the bottom of one bag. It will be gone within the first two days, so you clearly will have to reorganize this bag. Pack cheese packets on top and some of the longer lasting vegetables on top of the cheese. Pack the salad greens on the top of the bag. The meat, while it's frozen, will help to keep the other foods cool.

3. Pack similar foods in the same bag. Pack all the dry ingredients in one bag. If you've packaged zip lock bags with Bisquick, dried milk or the dry ingredients for other recipes, make sure that each bag is labeled in indelible ink, with instructions on a slip of paper inside for completing the recipe. Or, write the instructions directly on the baggie, again, using indelible ink. This includes dried soups, pastas and sauces.

4. Pack the hardy vegetables such as onions and cabbage at the bottom of a bag, carrots and cucumber, vertically to the sides. Pack the middle with other vegetables such as peppers, zucchini, herbs, garlic, shallots and such. Pack the container of fresh mushrooms or cherry tomatoes on the top.

5. Put the eggs on the top of a bag. Plastic egg containers to pack 6 or 12 eggs can be found at camping outfitters.

6. If you enjoy a glass of wine, buy a boxed wine. Remove the box and transport the bladder. Double bag it—you'll just have to buy another one and drink it at home before the trip! Slit the empty bag and remove the spout. Slip it over the full one and use duct tape to close the slits. These bags can also be purchased at some shops that sell camping or paddling gear. Then you can fill it with the wine of your choosing.

In the summer, Leslie and I enjoy a glass of cider. This should be bought in the two liter plastic containers available; not bottles. At the end of the trip, when the plastic bottle is empty, it can be crushed. You don't want empty glass bottles clunking around in your boat.

Port or sherry, for restoring spirits on cold, miserable days, should be poured into a Platypus® bag for easy transport.

If you enjoy a splash of rum or cognac in your coffee, bring a small metal flask.

If you like beer, you'll just have to deal with the empty cans. Make sure that you rinse them well, crush them, and put them in a sealed plastic bag.

As the trip progresses and you have enjoyed your fresh meat and some of your other wonderful taste treats, you will likely find yourself reorganizing your food stores to make for efficient packing. This is just the way it is on a paddling holiday.

Where's My Whisk?

Utensils

While the chef needs the ingredients to make the wonderful meals happen that have been planned for the trip, he or she also needs the tools to make it all work. I have laid out my list for the essentials to pack and other highly useful items to carry if you want to bake or be a little more luxurious with your food plans on your paddling holiday.

THE BASICS

- camp stove(s), fuel
- lighter, waterproof matches
- skillet—8–10 inch skillet with as heavy a bottom as you can accommodate, preferably with folding handle
- pots—stackable, with lids, attachable handle
- small wooden or hard plastic chopping board
- small wire whisk
- spatula—with or without folding handle
- good, sharp knife
- large spoon
- tongs
- plates, cutlery, bowls, mugs
- squares of aluminum foil to wrap up cut vegetables, cheese
- extra zip lock bags
- a bag for garbage
- biodegradable soap
- dish sponge and dish towels
- can opener, if necessary

IMPORTANT EXTRAS

- grater—small or rotary grater
- small rolling pin
- slotted spoon
- Italian coffee press
- shatterproof plastic wine glasses—the stem unscrews and tucks into the cup
- sheet of plastic 14–18 inches square for rolling out dough
- collapsible steamer to insert in a pot for steamed vegetables
- collapsible reflector oven or Dutch oven
- heat diffuser
- wok
- oyster shucker—if there's a possibility of gathering oysters

Although all of the recipes in this book include measurements for ingredients, you should be able to estimate or "eyeball" a quarter cup, a teaspoon, a gram and so forth. Measuring spoons and cups may be helpful to have along, but an experienced paddling chef should have the knowledge at hand to make the meals without having to measure all of the ingredients. Practice some recipes that appeal to you at home, so that you can prepare the meal easily in camp. Take your mug and your spoon and determine how much each holds. You really don't want to be reading a recipe card and fussing with measuring cups at your campsite!

Disasters of a Novice Camp Chef

Gambier Island, Howe Sound
Summer 1997

Since we began paddling three years ago, Leslie and I and our two young daughters have been expanding our kayaking experiences and are now confident that we can undertake a multi-day trip on our own. We will circumnavigate Gambier Island, heading out from Grafton Bay on Bowen Island. Brigade Bay, on the east coast of Gambier, is our destination for the first night.

Rounding the southeastern tip of Gambier, we feel a palpable change in emotions. Urban stresses slip away with every paddle stroke in the dark, glassy waters and our time-driven world is given over to Nature's agenda. We will be simple travelers along the way.

Our destination is Brigade Bay, part way up the east coast of Gambier. A small grassy area behind the storm-swept logs on the beach provides an ideal site for our first night's camp. We pitch the tent and begin to prepare dinner.

Fresh green salad and bacon were priorities on our grocery list when planning the food for this trip. The green salad is tied up and transported in a Safeway bag. Even with this short transport the salad greens are looking rather beaten up. We salvage a decent salad on this first evening but are left with a rapidly deteriorating bag of bruised greens.

There are few put in points on the west-coast of Gambier and many log booms are tethered to the shore. We asked permission and were granted the opportunity to camp at a deserted Catholic youth summer camp on the second night. The grassy volleyball court was a perfect site to pitch our tent, overlooking the sea and the caretaker's cabin.

The following morning, we are determined to have bacon and English muffins for breakfast. Our cooking stove is a large, metal, two-burner propane stove, more suitable for a canoe or camping trip; not a kayak excursion. It has been

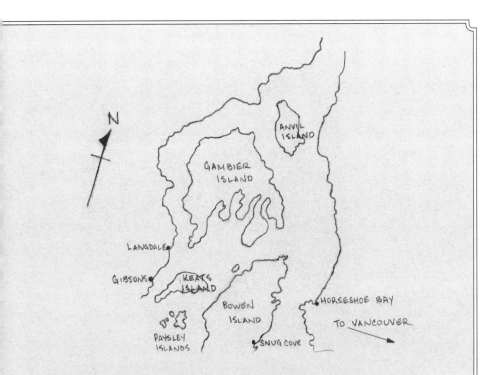

tucked in the front of my cockpit—the only place it could be stored—as it surely would not fit into a hatch.

Discovering that we've forgotten our frying pan, and with our inexperience in outdoor cooking, we decide to put the bacon strips directly on the grill of the camp stove. As the fat drips down and is ignited by the flames, we soon have a grand fire blazing. Turning off the propane and clamping the lid on the stove quickly smothers the flames on this culinary disaster. The charred, black remnants of the bacon are consigned to the Safeway bag along with the wilted lettuce.

My Christmas present from Leslie the following December was an efficient, pocket-sized Camping Gaz burner. It has been my kitchen companion ever since. A zip lock bag of Romaine lettuce, other hardy greens or a re-sealable bag of mixed greens will last for several days. We now take commercially prepared, precooked bacon strips that need no refrigeration, take only a minute to reheat and leave no fat.

Almost Like Home
MEAT

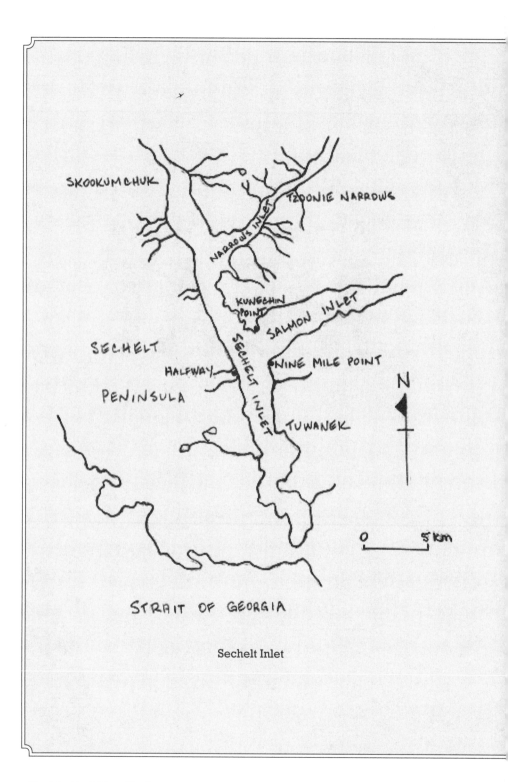

Sechelt Inlet

Sechelt Inlet
Summer, 1999

Leslie and I are paddling with our two young daughters up Sechelt Inlet to Narrows Inlet and back – a five-day trip.

The first day took us to Kunetchin Point on the north shore of Sechelt Inlet. After pitching our comfortable tent on the rocky promontory overlooking the confluence of Sechelt and Salmon Inlets, we set about assembling our kitchen on the sandy beach below. Two men were camped nearby, overlooking our kitchen site. We poured a glass of cider and opened the Camembert cheese to serve with crackers as we cooked our dinner - chicken breast on English muffins with Dijon mustard and salad. After dinner, as the aroma of freshly brewed coffee wafted up to them, the older of the two poked his head over the embankment.

"Do I smell coffee?"

"You are more than welcome to join us," we offered.

As we sat together with our coffee, pecan cookies and a glass of port, he expressed his surprise (and envy!) at the quality of our meal. Dinner for him and his son-in-law had been a brief affair, a "boil-in-the-bag" dinner in about ten minutes. They were traveling in a magnificent wooden canoe that he had built, which had a great capacity for storage—but they clearly missed the concept of fine dining on a beach.

Transporting Fresh Meat

If you decide to take fresh meat for the first one or two nights, transport it frozen, wrapped in tin foil and stored in a sealed plastic container. If you have a long drive to your put-in point, transport the frozen meat in a cooler with frozen potable water in plastic bottles that can later be used for drinking or cooking. Transfer the meat to a dry bag when you are ready to load. Canoeists and rafters can take a small cooler with frozen meat and ice packs in the boat itself and are therefore able to extend the opportunity to eat fresh meat.

Do not transport meat scraps in your garbage bag, as you will have to carry them for the remainder of the trip. They will rot along the way and attract any number of unwanted visitors, from wasps to bears. None of the meat recipes in this book leave any bones or skin as garbage. Dispose of any meat leftovers out in the lake, far from any source of drinking water, or in the sea. Row or paddle away from shore, but make sure that you do not contaminate your boat with the smell of the meat. Wash the container any meat has been in thoroughly with soap and hot water. This also applies to the chef: wash your hands well and don't sleep in clothes you have worn while cooking. Use a biodegradable soap such as Sea Suds, a product that works equally well in fresh or salt water.

The disposal of grey water is more problematic for a paddler on fresh water lakes or rivers than on the ocean. Although we humans most certainly have treated the ocean as a dumping ground for human and industrial waste, still the tidal flush and fish, crabs and other organisms in the sea are wonderfully efficient at dealing with organic matter that we dispose of in their environment. Paddlers on lakes or rivers have to be more careful, as lakes and rivers are the source of potable water for nearby communities. Strain the grey water of solid waste, vegetable or meat scraps. Then wastewater from cooking can be dumped in the bush. Dispose of grey water as far away from water sources as possible. Biodegradable bits of vegetables or meat strained off can be buried, but be careful when traveling in bear country.

As I've already mentioned, precooked bacon is a wiser choice over fresh bacon because there are no fat drippings in the pan to be dealt with after it's been heated. It also requires no refrigeration and can be part of the food stores for a long trip.

It is assumed that all the meats are thawed when preparing the recipes that follow.

CHICKEN

Fresh chicken should be eaten the first day.

Chicken and Red Onion Salad with Feta Cheese

DRESSING

- 1/2 cup (125 ml) olive oil
- 1/4 cup (60 ml) lemon juice
- 1/4 teaspoon (large dash) Tabasco sauce
- salt and pepper
- 1 teaspoon (5 g) oregano

The dressing can be prepared at home and transported in a small container.

SALAD

- 2 whole boneless, skinless chicken breasts, cut into thin strips
- 3 tablespoons (40 ml) olive oil
- 1 sweet red onion, sliced
- salad greens, approximately four cups
- crumbled feta cheese

In a skillet, heat the oil. Add the chicken and sauté for a few minutes. Add the onion. Continue cooking until the chicken is done and the onion is softened. Serve over a bed of salad greens. Crumble feta cheese on top and drizzle with the dressing.

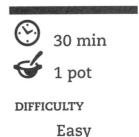

30 min

1 pot

DIFFICULTY

Easy

Serves 4

Variation:

For later in the trip, use a vacuum pack or can of tuna or can of chicken. Sturdy salad greens such as Romaine, endive, escarole, arugula and radicchio in a zip lock bag will last for several days.

Chicken with Mushrooms and Lemon Sauce

- 2 whole boneless, skinless chicken breasts, cut into thin strips
- 3 tablespoons (40 ml) olive oil
- 1 shallot, 2 garlic cloves
- 2 cups (500 g) sliced mushrooms
- handful of snow peas, trimmed
- 1 tbsp (15 ml) butter

30 min

1 pot

DIFFICULTY

Moderate

Serves 4

In a skillet, sauté chicken for five minutes in the olive oil. Add finely chopped shallot and garlic and continue cooking until the chicken is cooked and the shallot and garlic are soft, stirring often. Remove from pan, cover and set aside. Add the butter to the pan and cook the mushrooms and snow peas. Return the chicken to the pan.

LEMON SAUCE:

Combine these ingredients and drizzle over the chicken and vegetables.

- 1/4 cup (60 ml) chicken stock (use powdered bouillon or cube)
- A bouillon cube will make a cup of stock. Use the remainder when making the rice.
- 2 tablespoons (30 ml) white wine
- 2 tablespoons (30 ml) lemon juice
- 1 tablespoon (15g) finely chopped fresh rosemary or 2 teaspoons (10 g) dried rosemary

Toss to combine. Serve over rice.

Chicken Stir-Fry with Chutney

- 2 whole boneless, skinless chicken breasts, cut into thin strips
- 1/2 cup (120 ml) soy sauce
- 1 onion, sliced
- green pepper, sliced
- 3 tablespoons (40 ml) olive oil
- 1/2 cup (125 ml) mango or other chutney
- salt and pepper

🕐 30 min

🥣 1 pot

DIFFICULTY

Easy

Serves 4

Variation:

Other vegetables for stir fry:

Canned baby corn

Mushrooms

Snow peas

On a plate or pan, stir together the chicken breast strips and the soy sauce. Set aside to marinate. Meanwhile, sauté the onions and green pepper in a skillet with the oil. Remove from the skillet and keep warm. Reserving the marinade, cook the chicken slices in the skillet, adding a little more oil if needed. Add the vegetables and marinade. Stir in the chutney and season to taste with salt and pepper.

Serve with rice or couscous.

Chicken in Black Bean Sauce

- **boneless, skinless breast of chicken, cut into slices**
- **oil or ghee**
- **1 tablespoon (15 ml) soy sauce**
- **1 tablespoon (15 ml) black bean sauce**
- **1 tablespoon (20 g) corn starch**
- **1/2 teaspoon (2.5 g) sugar**
- **1 teaspoon (5 g) freshly grated ginger**
- **1/2 cup (125 ml) chicken stock or water**
- **1 small onion, coarsely chopped**

The first four ingredients for the sauce can be combined at home and transported in a small container. In camp, add the freshly grated ginger and the chicken stock or water.

In a skillet, sauté the slices of chicken in hot oil for a few minutes until the chicken is partly cooked. Add the onion and sauté with the chicken until the onion is softened. Combine all the sauce ingredients and add to the skillet. Stir for a few minutes until the sauce thickens and the chicken is cooked through.

Serve over rice.

30 min

2 pots

DIFFICULTY

Moderate

Serves 2

Variation:

Add chopped green pepper or snow peas.

Substitute fried tofu for the chicken.

Use the sauce to accompany fresh fish (but it's too heavy for trout and not suitable for salmon).

Chicken with Pasta, Tomatoes and Black Olives

- 3 cups (600 g) penne, rotini or other curly pasta
- 2 whole boneless, skinless chicken breasts, cut into strips
- 1/4 cup (60 ml) olive oil
- 1/2 cup (100 g) sliced black Italian olives
- 2 or 3 tomatoes, chopped
- 3 garlic cloves, finely chopped
- 1/2 teaspoon (2.5 g) thyme or oregano
- freshly ground pepper
- 1/2 cup (120 ml) white wine
- 3/4 cup (75 g) crumbled feta Romano or Parmesan cheese

Cook the pasta in a pot of boiling water. Meanwhile, sauté the garlic in the oil in a skillet. Add the chicken. Stir and cook until nearly done. Stir in the wine, cheese and spices. Add the olives and tomatoes. Stir the mixture as the cheese melts. Drain the pasta and add to the skillet. Toss the ingredients together.

Serve with salad or vegetables.

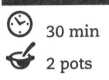

30 min

2 pots

DIFFICULTY

Moderate

Serves 4

Variation:

For later in the trip, use reconstituted olives, canned chicken or tuna, vacuum pack of tuna, can of tomatoes.

Omit the meat and use the pasta to accompany to fresh-caught fish or shellfish.

Easy Chicken Cordon Bleu

- 1 whole boneless, skinless chicken breast, cut in two pieces
- 2 slices of proscuitto or other dried, well-flavored ham
- 2 slices of Gruyère, Swiss or Emmenthal cheese
- 1 tbsp (15 ml) butter

Heat the butter in a skillet until bubbly. Add the chicken pieces. Sauté for several minutes. Turn over. Continue cooking for several more minutes or until the chicken is nearly done. Place a slice of ham and then a slice of cheese on each piece of chicken. Cover the pan and cook for three or four minutes until the chicken is cooked through and the cheese has melted. Serve with a creamy pasta or rice and vegetables.

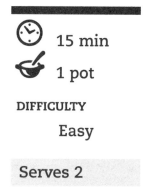

15 min

1 pot

DIFFICULTY

Easy

Serves 2

Picnic Chicken

This recipe has been in my family for years. It's just as tasty at room temperature and so has been the main course served on many picnics; hence its name. I have adapted it to use only boneless chicken breasts in keeping with my practice of not leaving any bones.

- **2 whole boneless, skinless chicken breasts, cut diagonally into thick slices**
- **1/2 cup (100 g) grated Parmesan cheese**
- **1/2 cup (100 g) dried bread crumbs**
- **1/4 cup (60 ml) butter**
- **1 teaspoon (5 g) garlic powder or two cloves minced garlic**
- **1 tablespoon (15 ml) Dijon mustard**
- **1 tablespoon (15 ml) Worcestershire sauce**

At home, combine the Parmesan cheese and bread crumbs in a zip lock bag.

In a small pot, melt the butter. Add the garlic, Dijon mustard and the Worcestershire sauce. Stir until well combined. Pour the liquid onto a plate or bowl. One by one, coat the chicken pieces with the sauce and toss in the bag with the crumb mixture.

Melt a little butter in a skillet. When the pan is quite hot, add the chicken pieces and sauté, turning pieces frequently until the chicken is cooked and the coating is browned, about 10 minutes. Turn down the heat if the chicken is browning too quickly.

If prepared in the manner I have described, the chicken pieces can be left to cool for a few minutes and eaten as finger food for an easy summer's dinner. Try dipping them in honey Dijon sauce and serve with a salad or raw vegetables such as carrots, green pepper, cucumber or cherry tomatoes and a chunk of buttered baguette.

🕐 **30 min**

🥄 **1 pot**

DIFFICULTY

Easy

Serves 4

Variation:

Cut the breasts in half (one piece per person) and serve with rice and vegetables. Drizzle a little of the liquid over the chicken when serving.

Nootka Island

August, 2000

Our trip this year will take us to Zeballos, a tiny community midway up Vancouver Island on the west coast, to begin our journey. Our first night will be spent at Mason's Lodge in Zeballos. We have afforded ourselves the luxury of having two fresh meat meals at the beginning of this trip, as our room at Mason's has a kitchen, and therefore, a freezer in the fridge.

Despite an early rising at 5:30, we don't launch until 10:00. We have to repack all our fresh and frozen food stores and drive to the launch site. This takes us considerably longer than expected because of the slow transport of the boats on the top of my car along the winding gravel road to the Causeway on Little Espinosa Inlet. The launch site is a mucky beach covered with mussels; not a pleasant access.

We try, unsuccessfully, to adjust the rudder pedals on our two rented single kayaks on the beach, but are anxious to get underway. This problem must be solved as soon as possible. As we head out, there is no wind and the seas are calm on Little Espinosa.

Our lunch stop is a small, pebbly beach on the eastern shore of Espinosa Inlet and we again turn our attention to the pedals. The wind is rising and we want to find a campsite at the tip of the mainland for the night. We ambitiously head out for our destination but soon find ourselves battling severe winds blowing up the inlet along with the incoming tide. As we are making no headway, we decide to turn back to the beach to wait out the wind. Although this is clearly the right decision, it also puts us in a precarious situation; turning the boats rudderless, against the wind.

Our stay of about three and a half hours on the beach is spent productively sorting out the rudder problems. We take time to absorb the special solitude

N

BROOKS PENINSULA

VANCOUVER ISLAND

BIG BUNSBY MARINE PARK

0 10Km

KYUQUOT

FAIR HARBOUR

ZEBALLOS

TAHSIS

RUGGED POINT

CATALA ISLAND

NOOTKA ISLAND

TO GOLD RIVER

YUQUOT (FRIENDLY COVE)

and the beauty of this
inlet. At about four o'clock
we head out again, hoping to get
established for the night before the fog,
which is rapidly advancing up Espinosa,
impedes our progress. The innocent little puffs
that chased each other up the inlet earlier in the day are being followed by an
ominous blanket rolling in over the coastal mountains from the sea.

Finally, landing on a reasonable stretch of beach as darkness begins to
fall, we find an excellent campsite behind a small stand of bushes. A
protected area adjacent will serve as our kitchen and dining area. We are
in bear country and will prepare meals well away from our tent site.
After setting up camp, we treat ourselves to a satisfying dinner of
chicken breast with stir-fried vegetables and rice; our reward after
an arduous and somewhat frustrating day.

BEEF

Frozen filets of beef or frozen ground beef should keep until the second day.

Filet of Beef

This is a luxury meal. But it's a great treat if you are a carnivore. If you want to be even more decadent, prepare a package of Béarnaise or Hollandaise sauce to serve with the steak.

- **2 medallions of beef filet**
- **olive oil**
- **Worcestershire sauce, steak sauce or steak spice**
- **packaged Béarnaise or Hollandaise sauce— check the package to make sure you have the necessary ingredients on hand to make the sauce.**

Heat a little olive oil in a skillet. Fry the steaks in the oil and brush with sauce or sprinkle steak spice on the meat when the meat is about half done. Turn in the pan two or three times until cooked to your liking.

Meanwhile, prepare the sauce according to the package instructions.

🕐 **30 min**

🥣 **2 pots**

DIFFICULTY

Easy

Serves 2

Accompaniments:

sautéed mushrooms, onions

salad or steamed vegetables

fried polenta, potatoes or pasta

Burritos with Ground Beef

This is a fun dinner to prepare on a lazy, beautiful evening, if you get everyone to lend a hand. It is easily modified to serve more paddlers or those with heartier appetites.

Have someone prepare the meat, another chop the vegetables and grate the cheese, and a third sauté the mushrooms. The fourth member can organize the plates and pour the wine.

We had burritos for dinner on our first overnight trip to Mayne Island and sat at our camp on Isle 240, sipping a glass of wine, the lights of Vancouver prominent to the east. But we knew that even at this short distance, we were well away from the city and our clock-driven lives.

- **1 pound (454 g) ground beef**
- **packet of taco seasoning**
- **1 cup (250 ml) water**
- **4, 8-inch soft tortillas (in a resealable package)**
- **1 cup (250 ml) salsa**
- **1 cup (250 ml) sour cream**
- **1/2 pound (.23 kg) chopped mushrooms**
- **3 tablespoons (45 ml) butter**
- **large tomato, diced**
- **lettuce, chopped**
- **1 cup (250 g) grated Cheddar or Monterey Jack cheese**

In a skillet, sauté the mushrooms in butter. Place in a bowl, cover and set aside.

Prepare the vegetables and cheese.

Break apart the meat and sauté in the skillet until well browned. Add the packet of seasoning and water according to the instructions. Stir until combined.

Put a measure of the meat down the middle of each tortilla. Layer the other ingredients on top in the order that the ingredients have been listed. Fold the top and bottom ends of the tortilla toward the center and roll up sideways, starting from one side. You will now have an enclosed package.

Serve with refried beans or guacamole.

⏱ **30 min**

🥄 **1 pot**

DIFFICULTY

Easy

Serves 2

Variation:

Substitute diced, cooked chicken breast for the beef

Rosa Island

The north shore of Nootka Island is a rugged place; the swells along the shore roar into sea caves. Suddenly, a head pops up out of the water only a few feet from Leslie's boat. Our first sea otter! He looks at us quizzically with his big, black eyes for a few moments, then gracefully arches his back and disappears under the surface. We round the northwest tip and head west toward our destination for the night, Rosa Island. Approaching the eastern shore of Rosa, we come upon a beautiful sandy bay, the first of many sandy beaches we will see while exploring the numerous small islands in the Nuchatlitz area. As we set up camp, we are happy to see another sea otter paddling leisurely on her back in the channel. We pitch our tent nestled against the trees with a view to the bay and east toward Nootka Island. There are several big logs nearby and one large, flat-topped one will serve very well as our kitchen. After settling in, we busy ourselves preparing our last fresh meat meal—filet of beef with sautéed mushrooms and onions, scalloped potatoes and salad with feta cheese. A glass of wine completes this bliss.

Variation: Vegetarian Burrito

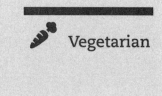

Vegetarian

To replace the meat, combine the ingredients together in a pot and heat.

- 1, 15 ounce can (475 ml) black beans, drained
- 1 cup (250 ml) chopped tomatoes
- 1 cup (250 ml) corn niblets
- 2 teaspoons (10 g) parsley, chopped
- 2 cloves garlic, finely chopped
- 1/2 teaspoon (2.5 g) chili powder or to taste
- 1/4 teaspoon (pinch) cayenne pepper or to taste

Serve with a salad, cucumber slices or sliced avocado.

Spicy Beef

Fish sauce is a key ingredient in the preparation of many Thai recipes. The fish sauce and coriander lend an exotic flavor to this dish. Soy sauce, combined with a dab of anchovy paste, can be substituted for the fish sauce.

- **16 ounces (.45 kg) filet of beef, transported frozen**
- **2 tablespoons (15 ml) olive oil**
- **2 teaspoons (3.5 ml) fish sauce**
- **1 onion, thinly sliced**
- **1 teaspoon (5 g) coriander**
- **3 tablespoons (45 ml) lemon juice**
- **1 tablespoon (15 g) sugar**

At home, combine the oil and fish sauce and transport in a film canister or other small container. Do the same with the coriander, lemon juice and sugar. In camp, coat the thawed beef with the oil and fish sauce and marinate for 15 to 30 minutes, turning several times. Cook the beef in a greased skillet until done to your liking. Remove from the pan and cover to keep warm. Fry the onions in the skillet, adding a little more oil if needed. Remove from the heat. Slice the beef diagonally into quarter-inch thick slices. Return the beef to the skillet with the onions. Add the dressing. Toss to combine.

Serve with raita, page 126, and pita or other flat bread with butter or ghee. Or serve with rice and a vegetable.

60 min

1 pot

DIFFICULTY

Moderate

Serves 2 to 4

Sausage-Tom-Dumps

When my mother, (the eldest of five children), was a young girl, she would make this dish to help her mother with the cooking. It's a hearty, one-pan meal. You will need a 10-inch skillet that you can cover for this recipe to work. It can be modified to serve two using an 8-inch skillet.

If you choose to take fresh sausages to serve early in the trip, transport them frozen like all other fresh meats. Although this recipe is listed under "Beef", you can use any type of sausages you like.

The dumpling recipe can be used on its own to accompany other meals.

- 1/2 cups (250 g) flour
- 4 teaspoons (20 g) baking powder
- 1/2 teaspoon (2.5 g) salt, pepper to taste
- 2 tablespoons (30 ml) butter
- 1 cup (250 ml) milk (made from powder)
- 12 fresh or precooked sausages, or dried sausages, reconstituted
- large can of crushed tomatoes or tomatoes with herbs, or the equivalent dried and reconstituted in camp

30 min

1 pot

DIFFICULTY

Moderate

Serves 4

Variation:

Add dried parsley flakes when preparing the dumplings.

Add one-quarter cup (50 g) grated Cheddar cheese to the dumpling dough.

Sauté green pepper slices with the sausages.

At home, combine the first three dry ingredients and transport in a zip lock bag. In camp, put the dry ingredients in a bowl. Cut in the butter with a fork. Add milk and combine to make a fluffy, slightly sticky dough.

If using dried sausages, reconstitute the sausages in a little water in a skillet. Simmer. Add more water until the sausages are plump. Drain any remaining water. Add the can or reconstituted tomatoes and simmer a few minutes, until the tomatoes are starting to bubble in the pan. With a spoon, divide the dumpling batter into eight individual dumplings and place on top of the sausage/tomato mixture. Cover the skillet and simmer for 10 to 15 minutes, or until dumplings are puffed and cooked through.

PORK

Pork tenderloin can be found in grocery stores, vacuum packed in plastic. It transports well frozen. If you can't find it vacuum-packed, prepare it as you would beef to transport.

Pork Tenderloin with Cinnamon Cran-Apple Sauce

- 1 1/2 pounds (700 g) pork tenderloin
- butter or oil
- 1 teaspoon (5 g) ground cinnamon
- 1 tablespoon (15 g) brown sugar
- 2 apples, peeled, cored and sliced or reconstituted apple sauce
- 2 tablespoons (30 g) dried cranberries or raisins

🕐 30 min

🥄 2 pots

DIFFICULTY

Moderate

Serves 4

Cook the pork tenderloin in a skillet with a little butter or oil. Turn every few minutes. Add a little more oil if necessary. The pork should be done in about twenty minutes.

Cook the apples in a small pot, stirring until softened, or warm the reconstituted apple sauce. Add the cranberries or raisins, brown sugar and cinnamon. Continue cooking until the apples have become applesauce and the raisins or cranberries are softened. Cover and set aside.

Cut the tenderloin diagonally into slices. Nap the pork slices with the sauce. Serve with fried potatoes or pasta and vegetables.

Pork Medallions with Mustard Sauce

- 3/4 pound (400 g) pork tenderloin
- 2 tablespoons (30 ml) olive oil

MUSTARD SAUCE
- 1 tablespoon (15 ml) butter
- 1 tablespoon (15 g) flour
- 1/2 cup (125 ml) milk (made from dry milk)
- 1/4 cup (60 ml) white wine
- 2 tablespoons (30 ml) Dijon mustard
- freshly ground pepper

Melt the butter in a small pan. Add the flour to make a roux. Stir for a few minutes until the flour is cooked. Add the milk and white wine, stirring constantly to make a medium sauce. Add the mustard. Continue cooking for a few more minutes. Add a little more water or wine if the sauce is too thick. Season with freshly ground pepper.

Slice the tenderloin into half-inch thick slices on the diagonal. Heat the skillet and add the oil. Cook the pieces of pork tenderloin for a few minutes on one side. Turn and cook until the pork is done, a few minutes more. Drizzle the tenderloin slices with the sauce.

30 min

2 pots

DIFFICULTY

Moderate

Serves 2

Variation:

Add 1 teaspoon (5 ml) horseradish

Add 1 teaspoon (5 ml) lemon juice

Pork Tenderloin with Dried Fruit

- 1 1/2 pounds (800 g) pork tenderloin
- 1/4 cup (60 ml) Worcestershire sauce
- 1/4 cup (60 ml) oil

Marinate the pork loin in the Worcestershire sauce for
fifteen minutes to half an hour, turning several times.

SAUCE:
- 1/4 cup (50 g) brown sugar
- 1/4 cup (60 ml) orange marmalade
- 1/4 cup (60 ml) beef broth
- 1/4 cup (60 ml) red wine
- 1/4 cup (50 g) dried apricots, chopped
- 1/4 cup (50 g) raisins

The first four ingredients for the sauce can be combined
at home and transported in a sealed container. In a small
pot, heat the first four ingredients. Add the apricots and
raisins. Stir and simmer over a low heat until the flavors
are combined and the fruits are softened. Be careful not to
burn the sauce. Add a little water if necessary.

Meanwhile, brown the pork tenderloin in a skillet with
a little oil. Turn every few minutes. Add some of the
marinade and continue cooking until the pork is done.
Slice the pork diagonally into half-inch thick slices.

*On individual plates, place slices of the pork over
cooked rice. Nap with the sauce.*

60 min

2 pots

DIFFICULTY

Moderate

Serves 4

Variation:

Substitute dried pineapple
tidbits or a small can of
drained tidbits for the
apricots. Use the liquid
from the can of pineapple
when making the rice.

Ham with Chanterelles in Hunter's Sauce

This is another hearty meal to prepare on a cool day and it's a wonderful dinner to enjoy late in a trip. It's one of my favorites when paddling with a small group.

- **tinned cooked ham**
- **2 tablespoons (30 ml) olive oil or butter**
- **small can or package of Hunter's sauce, or Hunter's sauce made at home, dried, reconstituted at camp, see page 155 153**
- **fresh or dehydrated chanterelle mushrooms, or other wild mushrooms, reconstituted**

Reconstitute dried mushrooms in water or wine for 30 minutes. Chop and add to the Hunter's sauce. Heat in a small saucepan. In a skillet, sauté ham in oil until heated through and browned. Serve with the sauce.

Serve this meal accompanied by sautéed cabbage and garlic mashed potatoes.

🕐 **60 min**

🥄 **1 pot**

DIFFICULTY

Moderate

Serves 4

Variation:

More complicated, but you will impress your paddling companions. If you can't find prepared Hunter's sauce, it can be made at home, dried, and reconstituted at camp.

Ham and Pineapple with Sweet and Sour Sauce

- **can of ham, cut into quarter-inch thick slices**
- **olive oil or butter**
- **small can of crushed pineapple**
- **1 green pepper, sliced**
- **1 onion, sliced**
- **1/2 cup (125 ml) sweet and sour sauce**

Sauté the green pepper and onion in butter or olive oil in a skillet. Add the can of pineapple. Remove, cover and keep warm. Sauté the slices of ham. On a separate burner, warm the sweet and sour sauce in a small pot. Place the ham slices, topped with the vegetables, on plates. Add the sweet and sour sauce.

Serve with rice.

⏱ 15 min

🥣 2 pots

DIFFICULTY

Easy

Serves 4

Variation:

Add sautéed mushrooms

FISH & SHELLFISH

Although fish or shellfish would never be transported from home on a paddling trip, bottom feeders like rockfish can be easily caught with just a line and a little fresh bait. Look for mussels, large barnacles or bits of your own food to use as bait. All you need is a piece of wood with a line wound around it and a hook on the end. If you're in a kayak, place a garbage bag or other piece of plastic on the deck in front of the cockpit. Take a hard piece of wood or commercially made fish bonker to dispatch the fish when you pull it onboard the kayak. It's not pretty, but do you want fresh fish for dinner?

Fishing from a canoe or raft with a trolled lure is an easier process, as the paddler is not sealed in a cockpit with a sprayskirt and can move about more easily. However, it's not a good idea to bring fish inside, as the smell could attract bear on shore. Keep your catch on a stringer or in a fish bag in the water, or put the fish in a plastic container in the boat.

Fish slime should be kept from clothing and hands and dishes should be washed thoroughly. Taking clothing you've worn when preparing food into the tent could bring you an unwanted, furry tent-mate.

Clean your catch well away from your campsite. We humans have a poor sense of smell, but this isn't the case for most other animals, especially raccoons and bears. Throw the guts, bones and any other remains from your catch out into the sea, to be washed away by the tide. On a lake, if necessary, paddle out into deep water away from camp. On a river, dispose of the fish scraps down river from where you want to draw water. In other words, treat fresh caught remnants as you would other fresh meat remains on a paddling trip.

I have never fished for salmon from a kayak, but I know it's possible. One would need to be a confident fisher as well as kayaker to undertake this endeavor. Salmon are fighters, and landing one will test both skills. Salmon were leaping out of the water all over the place in Johnstone Strait near the Broughton Archipelago and I was salivating at the thought of fresh salmon for dinner. Maybe one day I'll make the effort.

Freshly caught fish are delicious simply sautéed in butter and drizzled with lemon but I have included several recipes for sauces that are particularly good with fish in Chapter Eight.

Bivalves such as oysters and clams can be found on beaches, and mussels are often found attached to rocks or rocky outcrops. Oysters are a challenge, as you really should have a proper shucking knife along if you expect to find these exceptional treats on an ocean adventure. As with mushrooms, foraging for bivalves has to be undertaken with care. Many coastal areas are closed due to pollutants or the threat of paralytic shellfish poisoning. As these animals are filter feeders, they readily retain toxins in their bodies. After cooking, discard unopened bivalves. They're already dead and shouldn't be eaten.

Check with the local authorities (Fisheries Canada or the American Fish and Wildlife Service) before gathering any shellfish for dinner. If renting a boat in the area you plan to travel, the proprietors of the rental shop should be able to give you the appropriate information. Always make sure you've bought any required fishing licenses.

Should you be so fortunate to catch fish or gather oysters, clams or mussels, here are a few preparation and serving suggestions.

Clams or Mussels Steamed in White Wine

- 2 pounds (1 kg) fresh clams or mussels
- 1 tablespoon (15 ml) butter
- 1 large shallot, finely chopped
- 2 garlic cloves, finely chopped
- freshly ground pepper
- 1/4 cup (60 ml) water
- 1/2 cup (125 ml) white wine

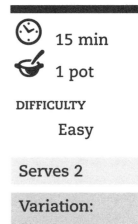

15 min

1 pot

DIFFICULTY

Easy

Serves 2

Variation:

Add chopped chorizo, chopped tomato and a sprinkle of your favorite herb to the pot when adding the shellfish.

Clean the clams or mussels of any debris on the shell. Melt the butter in a pot and sauté the shallot and garlic for a few minutes until soft. Add the water and wine to the pot. Season with salt and pepper. Add the shellfish. Cover, bring to a boil and steam for 7 to 10 minutes until the shells open. Discard any unopened shells. Divide between two bowls, or just enjoy directly from the pot.

Serve with salad or raita (page 126)

Breaded Oysters

This is the same recipe as Picnic Chicken.

- **4 pounds (2 kg) oysters in the shell**
- **1/2 cup (100 g) grated Parmesan cheese**
- **1/2 cup (100 g) dried bread crumbs**
- **1/4 cup (60 ml) butter, melted**
- **1 teaspoon (15 ml) Dijon mustard**
- **1 teaspoon (15 ml) Worcestershire sauce**
- **freeze dried parsley (optional)**

Shuck the oysters and remove the meat from the shell. Combine the melted butter, mustard and Worcestershire sauce. Coat the oysters with the butter, then with the Parmesan and bread crumb mixture. Sauté in a skillet with a little butter (or even better, ghee—page 157) for a few minutes, turning once.

15 min

2 pots

DIFFICULTY

Easy

Serves 4

Variation:

Oysters on the half shell. Shuck the oysters but leave the meat in the heavier, curved half of the shell. Halve the amount of butter when preparing the butter sauce. Drizzle a little of the butter mixture over each oyster. Halve the crumb mixture. Sprinkle a little of the crumb mixture on top of each oyster. Sprinkle with a little freeze dried parsley. Place the oysters in their shells on a heated skillet. Cover and cook for a few minutes until the sauce bubbles.

Serve with slices of baguette or chunks of English muffin to dip up the sauce.

Oysters on the Half Shell with Ginger and Garlic

- 4 pounds (2 kg) oysters in the shell
- 2 garlic cloves, finely chopped
- 1 tablespoon (15 g) grated ginger or 1 teaspoon (5 g) ground ginger
- 1 green onion, finely chopped
- 1/4 cup (60 ml) soy sauce
- 2 tablespoons (30 ml) butter
- 1/4 cup (60 ml) white wine

Melt the butter in a skillet and sauté the garlic until softened. Add the ginger and green onion. Cook for a minute or two. Add the soy sauce and wine. Heat through.

Prepare the oysters as described in the variation for Breaded Oysters, above. Drizzle the sauce over the oysters, place in a skillet and cook as for Breaded Oysters.

15 min

2 pots

DIFFICULTY

Easy

Serves 4

Variation:

Use this sauce to enhance any fish you have caught.

The Staples

PASTA, RICE & BREADS

Carbohydrates provide the base for many a paddler's dinner, or are served as a welcome accompaniment to protein and vegetables. A lot of calories are expended on a paddling/camping journey. Carbohydrates are needed to maintain energy reserves for those long or arduous paddling days when you find yourself battling wind, waves, tides, and currents.

Breads that Travel Well on a Watery Adventure

English muffins are virtually indestructible. Plain and sourdough muffins are excellent for constructing the base for breakfasts such as Eggs Benedict, fried eggs and ham, easy sandwiches for lunches, or garlic toast to accompany dinner. Raisin English muffins with jam make a simple, tasty breakfast when an early start in the morning is important. Otherwise, they're a lovely afternoon treat with a cup of tea after landing in the afternoon and establishing camp.

Crumpets will also travel well. Warmed in a skillet and buttered with jam, served with orange segments, they're an easy breakfast.

Pita, naan, pappadams, and tortillas are also great staples and will last a week or more. Pita can be stuffed with veggies and meats or simply pulled apart and buttered. Pita, naan and pappadams can be dipped into a small dish of balsamic vinegar and olive oil, served for an al fresco lunch on the beach, with sliced sausage, cheese and fruit. Soft tortillas can be made into wraps for easy lunches or dinners.

Baguette. Take on the first day to eat at lunch. Make French toast with leftovers for breakfast the next morning, garlic toast for dinner, or croutons for a hearty salad.

Dry Ingredients to Prepare in Camp

Bisquick. Use the instructions on the box of Bisquick (or other mixes) to prepare packages of the dry ingredients in zip lock bags at home to make pancakes, cheese biscuits, cinnamon raisin rolls, Parmesan garlic biscuits and the like. Include a slip of paper with instructions for preparing at camp and label the zip lock bag with a permanent marker.

Bannock. This sturdy bread is a staple of the First Nations Peoples. There are dozens of recipes for bannock and the proportions of the ingredients vary considerably. Bannock can be heavy and dry. I have included two recipes that are lighter and adaptable.

Crêpes are easy to make and can be stuffed with a wide variety of ingredients. They make quite an elegant presentation served with fresh steamed vegetables or a salad.

Other Important Carbohydrates

Pasta and rice provide the foundation for many a paddler's meal. Dried pasta and rice are light-weight foods to pack. There are endless varieties of dried pasta available at an Italian grocery. Small or curly ones are easiest to use—shell pasta, fusilli, rotini, lumache ("snails"), farfalle and penne—but spaghetti isn't a problem to transport if it's properly packed. If using dry bags, put the spaghetti in the cardboard tube left over from a roll of paper towels, or break it in half and do the same with a toilet paper roll. Wrap in plastic wrap or foil. Pack it in the middle of a dry bag, or store the spaghetti in one of your plastic containers. Dried, stuffed pastas such as tortellini can also be found at Italian markets.

Couscous, the staple dish of Morocco, Algeria and Tunisia, is also easily found at the local grocery.

Risotto, made with Arborio rice, is the base for an excellent meal to which a variety of ingredients can be added.

Commercially prepared packages with dried sauces are great to have on hand for those days when preparing a more leisurely meal is problematic due to time or weather. These can be augmented with a can or vacuum pack of tuna, chicken or chopped ham, bacon or sausage and a variety of vegetables. Although we pride ourselves in eating well, we don't want to beat ourselves up over food. Sometimes, the easy way out is just fine.

Dried Asian noodles such as ramen can be supplemented with mushrooms, egg, bits of broccoli, or ham for an easy dinner after a late landing, or a hot lunch on a stormy day.

Mein noodles are easily substituted for rice to make a stir fry meal.

Japanese clear noodles, made from mung beans, while taking more time to prepare, and somen—thin, Japanese wheat noodles—can provide the base for a meal prepared by a more adventurous paddling chef.

Potatoes travel well and are easy to prepare in a variety of ways, although bulk and weight must be considered. Take small new potatoes or thin-skinned potatoes, such as Yukon Gold, that don't need to be peeled. Potatoes can be fried, boiled, mashed, or made into potato salad. Milk, butter, sour cream, cream cheese, garlic, Dijon mustard and herbs can be added to enhance the flavor of potatoes, or sprinkle them with dried bacon bits.

Gnocchi, made from potatoes, but treated much like pasta, is also easy to transport.

Polenta, a roll of corn meal, is an interesting addition to the carb pack. Fried slices can accompany a meal or serve as an appetizer, before a leisurely-prepared dinner, with a glass of wine. Unrefrigerated, prepared rolls of polenta are readily available in most supermarkets. After it's been opened, refrigeration is required, but it can be a great addition for later in a trip and will still keep for a few days if temperatures are cool at night.

BREADS

Pizza Dough

- 1 tablespoon yeast (1 packet)
- 1 teaspoon (7 g) salt
- 1 tablespoon (15 g) sugar
- 1 tablespoon (15 ml) olive oil
- 1/2 cup (125 ml) warm water
- 1 1/2 cups (375 g) flour

60 min

1 pot

Vegetarian

DIFFICULTY

Easy

Combine the first five ingredients in a pot or bowl. Let sit for five minutes. Gradually add the flour, stirring to combine. Remove from the pot and knead on a smooth surface for several minutes. (Take along a small sheet of flexible plastic, about 18 inches square, for this purpose.) Cover and let rise for an hour. Punch down. Divide the dough in two. Form a ball and roll out into a circle about ¼ inch thick, to fit your skillet.

Place the dough in a greased skillet, pressing the dough out to the edges of the pan. Spread the dough with tomato sauce. Add cooked, sliced mushrooms; pepperoni or salami slices; smoked salmon; capers; sliced olives; chopped onions or green peppers; or any other ingredient you like. The possibilities are endless. Top with shredded mozzarella, Parmesan, Cheddar, or feta cheese.

Cook over medium heat until the bottom of the pizza is lightly browned, the toppings are heated through and the cheese is melted, about 10 minutes. If necessary, cover to melt the cheese. Make sure not to burn the bottom of the pizza crust. A heat diffuser is great to have on hand for recipes like this.

If you're paddling on a short trip and don't want to be bothered making the dough in camp, pizza crusts can be bought at most grocery stores. Individual-sized ones are easier to take on a kayak trip, but a large one can be taken on a canoe trip. Just make sure it's not too big for your skillet, or pack a round, flat baking sheet in the bottom of your kitchen bag.

Crêpe Batter

- 3/4 cup (150 g) flour
- pinch salt
- 2 eggs
- 3/4 cup (90 ml) milk
- butter or oil

15 min

1 pot

Beat the eggs. Combine flour and salt. Add eggs to flour and add enough milk to make a runny batter. Grease an 8-inch skillet and pour about a quarter-cup of batter into the pan. Roll the skillet to evenly distribute the batter. Cook for a few minutes, until the edges of the crêpe begin to curl. Turn, or, if you're adventurous and want to show off your culinary skills, shake the pan and flip the crêpe. Cook briefly on the other side. Remove from the pan, and stack the crêpes on a plate. Cover to keep warm. Grease the pan as needed as you cook the rest of the crêpes. Makes 4-5 crêpes.

DIFFICULTY

Easy

Serves 2 to 4

Pancakes

I use Bisquick mix to make pancakes.
It's easy and works well.

- **2 cups (400g) Bisquick mix**
- **2 eggs**
- **1 cup (250 ml) milk**

Put the Bisquick mix into a bowl. In another bowl, lightly
beat the eggs. Add the eggs and milk to the Bisquick. Stir
gently to combine. The batter should be fluffy.

Drop a scant quarter-cup of batter for each pancake on a
greased, heated skillet. A drop of water should sizzle if
your pan is hot enough. You'll have to watch carefully that
the pan doesn't get too hot or you'll have hockey pucks
instead of golden pancakes.

15 min
1 pot

DIFFICULTY

Easy

Serves 4

Variation:

If you've found fresh
berries, add them to the
batter or sprinkle on top.

Serve with maple
syrup or drizzle with
lemon juice mixed with
powdered sugar.

Accompany with fried,
precooked bacon or
reconstituted sausages.

Easy Cheddar Herbed Biscuits

These can be made at home and will keep for a few days while traveling. Or, if you have a collapsible reflector oven and the time, the biscuits can be made in camp.

- 2 1/4 cups (450 g) Bisquick mix
- 1/2 cup (100 g) grated Cheddar cheese
- 2 teaspoons (10 g) dried herbs (basil, rosemary or parsley)
- 1/4 cup (60 ml) sour cream
- 2 tablespoons (30 ml) Dijon mustard
- 1/3 cup (80 ml) milk
- 1 egg, lightly beaten

At home: Preheat oven to 425°F. (220°C.) In a medium bowl, mix together the Bisquick mix, cheese and herbs. In a separate bowl, combine the sour cream, mustard and milk. Stir into the dry ingredients until well combined. Drop the dough in two-inch rounds onto a greased baking sheet. Brush tops with beaten egg. Bake for 12 to 15 minutes.

In camp: Prepare the batter as above. Arrange your collapsible oven over the skillet and preheat to 325°F. (170°C.) Remove the cover. Grease the skillet. Drop the batter in smaller rounds than you would at home onto the skillet. Replace the cover and bake for 8 minutes. You will have to make two batches, as the skillet is smaller than a baking sheet.

Baking in camp is a tricky business; the biscuits bake quickly over a burner. The paddling chef may have to experience some hockey pucks before getting the feel of baking with a collapsible camp oven.

🕑 **30 min**

🥄 **1 pot**

DIFFICULTY
Moderate

Makes approximately 16 biscuits

Dead Simple Cheese Biscuits

- **English muffins, split**
- **butter**
- **dried herbs**
- **grated Cheddar cheese**

Mix together the herbs and the butter. Let sit for a few minutes to combine the flavors. Butter the English muffins. Sprinkle with the grated cheese. Place on a skillet over low heat and cover with a lid. Enjoy when the cheese has melted.

15 min

1 pot

DIFFICULTY

Easy

Cheesy Pita Bread

- **1 piece pita bread, sliced open sideways**
- **2 tablespoons (30 ml) butter**
- **1 garlic clove, finely chopped**
- **parsley flakes**
- **crumbled feta cheese**

Mix together the butter, garlic, parsley and feta cheese. Spread in pita pocket. Place in heated skillet. Turn after a few minutes. The pita should be slightly browned and the cheese warm and soft. Cut the pita in half to serve.

15 min

1 pot

DIFFICULTY

Easy

Serves 2

Calzones

This recipe for a pizza turnover is not difficult to make and serve but take care that the dough is well sealed or you'll have a great mess on your hands when you turn the calzone. This is a fun meal to brag about to your land-loving friends. It's a good meal to use up leftover bits of vegetables.

Recipe for pizza dough, page 71.

Roll out the dough to the size of your pan on a piece of plastic. Add ingredients as you would for a pizza, using tomato sauce, tomatoes, cheese, chopped sausage, canned fish, chopped onions, mushrooms or any other ingredients that you choose and place on one half of the dough. Fold over and seal by crimping the edges together. Rub a little water, if necessary, to seal the dough. You should have a half-pie shaped, stuffed piece of dough when you're done.

Grease a skillet with butter or olive oil. Sauté the calzone on low heat for several minutes until browned. Turn over and cover the pan. Sauté for several more minutes until browned on the other side. The stuffing should be heated through and the cheese melted. Cut in half to serve for two.

60 min

1 pot

Vegetarian

DIFFICULTY

Moderate

Serves 2

Garlic Toast

- **French bread, in thick slices or English muffins, halved**
- **butter or olive oil**
- **garlic—finely chopped cloves, or powdered garlic**

Combine the garlic and butter in a small dish. Generously butter the French bread or muffins. Toast, buttered side down, in a skillet and cook until slightly browned.

15 min

1 pot

Vegetarian

DIFFICULTY

Easy

Bannock

- 1 cup (225 g) flour
- 3 teaspoons (15 g) baking powder
- 1/2 teaspoon (2.5 g) salt
- 1 tablespoon (15 g) sugar
- 3 tablespoons (45 ml) butter
- 1/2 cup (125 ml) water

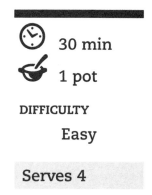

30 min

1 pot

DIFFICULTY

Easy

Serves 4

Combine the dry ingredients at home and put into a zip lock bag. Add the butter and cut in with a fork to form a crumbly mixture. Add the water to the flour mixture and combine to form a soft dough. Knead the dough on a flat surface for a minute or two until smooth. Use a plate or the same piece of plastic you used to make your pizza dough. Form into four patties about one half-inch thick.

Heat a skillet over the burner. Add a knob of butter and heat until just bubbly. Place the patties in the pan and
cook until browned and crusty. Turn. Cover the pan and cook the other side for a few minutes, until the dough is cooked through.

Add freshly picked berries to the recipe, if you're lucky enough to find some. Another option is to add one-quarter cup (50 g) grated Cheddar cheese or crumbled bits of feta cheese to the batter.

Bannock—A Cree Recipe

- 1 1/2 cups (300 g) flour
- 2 teaspoons (10 g) baking powder
- pinch of salt
- 1/4 cup (60 ml) butter
- 3/4 cup (125 - 150 ml) water—
  enough water to make a soft dough
- 1/4 cup (50 g) currants or raisins

30 min

1 pot

DIFFICULTY

Easy

Serves 4

Prepare as for the first bannock recipe. Add the currants or raisins to the batter before cooking. This recipe has a heavier consistency.

Variation: Bannock Cinnamon Rolls

The bannock recipe can be used to make cinnamon rolls for breakfast. Roll out the dough into a rectangle one-quarter inch thick. Use a nice piece of wood found at camp or, in a pinch, the shaft of your paddle. This could create a great photo op! Don't even think of transporting a regular rolling pin unless you expect to have a serious altercation with one of your paddling companions en route! Small rolling pins can be found at specialty kitchen shops—or just cut an eight inch piece of one-inch dowel and sand the ends smooth.

MIX TOGETHER:

- 1/4 cup (25 g) brown sugar
- 1/2 cup (50 g) butter, softened
- 1 teaspoon (5 g) cinnamon
- 1/4 teaspoon (2.5 g) nutmeg
- 1/2 cup (100 g) raisins or currants
- 1/4 cup (50 g) finely chopped walnuts

Spread the mixture evenly over the dough. Roll up. Cut into one-inch thick slices. Place the buns on a skillet or pot and bake in a reflector oven at 350°F. for 15 or 20 minutes.

Serve with apple slices, pieces of pineapple, orange segments, or other fruits on hand.

Parathas

Indian parathas are unleavened, like other simple staple breads made all over the world. They can be prepared in several ways, using the basic recipe or stuffed with a wide variety of ingredients. They are often served in India as a practical and tasty way for using up leftovers from the fridge, or in this case, camp. If you find yourself with half an onion or green pepper, four or five mushrooms, the last bit of cheese or a tomato that will not last another day, preparing parathas is a great way of making a productive meal instead of letting the leftovers wither away to be consigned to the garbage bag.

Traditionally, parathas are served early in the day, as a breakfast or brunch meal but serve them any time you wish in camp. I have included three recipes to demonstrate the ways that parathas can be served, but this is one dish where you really can use your imagination, adding favorite herbs and spices to the ingredients at hand.

Basic Parathas

- 2 cups (100 g) flour, extra flour for rolling out the dough
- 1 tablespoon (15 ml) oil or ghee
- 1/4 teaspoon (pinch) salt
- 1/2 cup (125 ml) water

60 min

1 pot

Vegetarian

DIFFICULTY

Easy

Serves 2

Mix the first three ingredients together in a bowl. Add the water a little at a time until a soft dough is formed. Knead for a few minutes. Cover with a damp cloth and let sit for 20 to 30 minutes.

Take a golf-ball sized piece of dough and roll out on a lightly floured piece of plastic to form a circle about 6 inches in diameter. Brush with oil or ghee. Fold in half. Roll again. Brush with more of the oil you are using and fold again. You will now have a piece of dough that looks like a squashed cone or a quarter of a circle. Heat the oil in a skillet. Add the parathas two or three at a time, depending on the size of your skillet, and cook until sizzling and browned. Turn and cook the other side.

Serve with an omelette or frittata, dip into chutney or yogurt or just enjoy them, hot and buttery, by themselves.

The following two recipes are other ways to serve parathas. Use them as jumping off points to challenge your chef's creativity and use up your leftovers.

Stuffed Parathas Version 1

BASIC PARATHA DOUGH
- 2 cups (100 g) flour, extra flour for rolling out the dough
- 1 tablespoon (15 ml) oil or ghee
- 1/4 teaspoon (pinch) salt
- 1/2 cup (125 ml) water

FILLING:
- 1/2 cup (125 ml) tomato, seeded and finely chopped
- 1 cup (200 g) onion, finely chopped
- 1 teaspoon (10 g) dried coriander
- 1 teaspoon (10 g) red chili powder
- 1/2 teaspoon (5 g) cumin
- salt, to taste

60 min

1 pot

Vegetarian

DIFFICULTY

Easy

Serves 2

Make the batter according to the directions for basic parathas.

Combine the ingredients for the filling. Roll the parathas out to a diameter of 4 inches. Add a measure of the filling in the middle—a tablespoon or so. Fold up the edges of the dough around the filling rather like a Hershey's Kiss, overlapping the edges. Press the edges together gently.

Carefully roll out the stuffed dough to 6 inches in diameter. Cook the stuffed parathas as you would the basic parathas. Serve while crisp and hot with raita (cucumber salad) or mirch achaar (chili pickles).

Stuffed Parathas Version 2

BASIC PARATHA DOUGH
- 2 cups (100 g) flour, extra flour for rolling out the dough
- 1 tablespoon (15 ml) oil or ghee
- 1/4 teaspoon (pinch) salt
- 1/2 cup (125 ml) water

FILLING:
- One-half a small cabbage, shredded
- 2 teaspoons (20 g) grated ginger
- 2 green chilies, finely chopped
- 1 teaspoon (10 g) dried coriander

60 min

1 pot

Vegetarian

DIFFICULTY

Easy

Serves 2

Make the dough according to the directions for basic parathas.

Combine the ingredients for the filling. Divide the batter into two pieces. Roll out into two rounds on a floured sheet. Spread one half of the filling onto half of the paratha. Fold the other half over to form a "D" shaped piece of dough. Sprinkle the edges with a little water and crimp with your finger or a fork to seal.

Cook in the same manner as already described.

Cut the paratha in half to serve.

Japanese Pancake or Pizza

In Japanese, this is called "okonomiyaki," which translates to "as you like it." So, like other dough-based recipes, all kinds of ingredients can be added to suit your own taste. It can be served using just the following recipe to accompany meat or fish, or as a meal as itself.

- **2 1/2 cups (500 g) flour**
- **3/4 cup (170 ml) water**
- **2 eggs**
- **1/2 cup (100 g) cabbage, shredded**
- **butter or oil**

Lightly beat the eggs. Combine the flour and water. Add a little more water if necessary to make a soft dough. Add the eggs and cabbage. Divide the mixture in two to make two pancakes. Press into a greased skillet and sauté for a minute or two. Turn over. Treat the okonomiyaki as you would a round of pizza dough.

🕐 **15 min**

🥣 **1 pot**

DIFFICULTY

Moderate

Serves 2 to 4

Regional Variations:

Hiroshima Style
Add tomato sauce, finely chopped onion, flakes of tuna or chicken, herbs or other ingredients, finely chopped to your taste. Cover the skillet and cook until heated through—one or two minutes.

Osaka Style
To make the okonomiyaki in the Osaka style, combine the ingredients you want to add into the dough (not tomato sauce). Press onto the skillet. Then cook until lightly browned. Turn over and cook the other side.

Serve with okonomi sauce, available at Japanese markets, to impress your fellow paddlers.

Risotto with Zucchini

If pasta is the important carbohydrate for recipes in southern Italy, risotto is the staple for the north. It's often served as a first course but on a paddling/camping adventure it provides a wonderful base for a main dish. While somewhat time-consuming to make and requiring the constant attention of the chef, the basic recipe is simple. Pour a glass of wine while you sit and stir.

- 2 zucchini, thinly sliced
- 6 tablespoons (90 ml) butter
- 4 slices precooked bacon, diced
- 1 medium onion, finely chopped
- 4 cloves garlic, finely chopped
- 1 tablespoon (15 g) freeze-dried parsley (optional)
- 2 1/2 cups (500 g) Arborio rice
- 5 cups (1.25 liters) beef bouillon
- 3/4 cup (185 ml) white wine
- 1/2 cup (100 g) Parmesan cheese
- salt and freshly ground pepper

60 min

1 pot

DIFFICULTY

Easy

Serves 4 to 6

Melt the butter in a pot large enough to accommodate the rice and bouillon. (Remember that your rice will double in bulk by the end of cooking time.) Sauté the onion, garlic and bacon until the onion is softened and golden. Add the zucchini and cook for a few minutes until the zucchini is browned. Add the rice. Cook for a few minutes, stirring all the time. Add the parsley. Add the bouillon one cup at a time until it's absorbed, approximately 20-25 minutes. Season with salt and pepper. Stir in the Parmesan. Let the risotto sit for a couple of minutes before serving.

All sorts of ingredients—meat, fish, chicken or other vegetables—can be added near the end of cooking to make a one-pot meal.

Polenta with Onion, Herbs and Tomatoes

- 4 slices of polenta, cut one-quarter inch thick
- 2 tablespoons (30 ml) olive oil
- 2 tablespoons (30 ml) butter
- 1 teaspoon (5 g) Italian herbs
- 2 garlic cloves, chopped
- 1/2 cup (100 g) onion, chopped
- 2 plum tomatoes, chopped
- grated Parmesan or Asiago cheese

In a skillet, sauté the garlic and onion in butter. Add the chopped tomatoes and the herbs. Stir and cook until the tomatoes are soft. Remove from the pan, cover and keep warm. Brush the slices of polenta with olive oil. Sauté in the skillet for 2 or 3 minutes per side until slightly browned. Serve topped with the tomato and onion mixture and sprinkled with the cheese.

15 min

1 pot

Vegetarian

DIFFICULTY

Easy

Serves 2

Variation:

¼ cup (50 g) diced green peppers

1 tablespoon (15 g) chopped sun-dried tomatoes

½ teaspoon (2.5 g) basil

½ cup (125 g) feta cheese

Sauté the green pepper in butter or oil. Add the sun-dried tomatoes and basil. Add the feta cheese and stir until melted. Spoon onto the cooked polenta.

Glass Noodle Salad

- 8 ounces (200 g) glass noodles
  (available at Asian markets)
- 1 cup (200 g) ground beef,
  or dried equivalent, reconstituted
- 4 green onions, cut into 1 inch long pieces
- 2 medium tomatoes, chopped
- juice of one lime
- 2 tablespoons (30 ml) oil

SAUCE:
- 1 tablespoon (15 g) brown sugar
- 1/2 teaspoon (5 g) chili paste
- 3 tablespoons (45 ml) soy sauce
- 1 tablespoon (15 ml) fish sauce
- 1 tablespoon (15 ml) sesame oil

30 min

1 pot

DIFFICULTY

Moderate

Serves 3 or 4

Combine the five ingredients for the sauce at home and transport in a small plastic container.

Soak the noodles in warm water for 10 minutes. Drain and wash with a little cold water. Cut the noodles into smaller pieces.

Heat a little oil in a skillet. Add the green onions and the beef. Cook until the beef is hot and the onions are softened, stirring frequently. Remove from the heat. Add the glass noodles and the tomatoes. Add the juice of one lime and the sauce ingredients. Toss together.

Chow Mein

- 6 tablespoons (90 ml) olive oil or butter
- 3 tablespoons (45 g) garlic, finely chopped
- 1 small onion, coarsely chopped
- 1/2 cup (125 ml) chicken or vegetable broth
- 2 baby bok choi, cut in half
- 12 ounces (375 g) chow mein noodles
- 1/2 cup (125 ml) soy sauce

Heat the oil in a skillet. Sauté the garlic and onion until the onion is softened and browned. Add the broth and heat until boiling. Add the chow mein noodles. Stir constantly. Add the soy sauce. Continue stirring. Add the bok choi. Cover the skillet and cook for a few minutes until the bok choi is steamed, but still crisp.

30 min

1 pot

Vegetarian

DIFFICULTY

Easy

Serves 2

Variation:

Slivers of ham, pieces of tuna or chicken

Add fresh or rehydrated mushrooms

Substitute green pepper, broccoli or cabbage for the bok choi

Rotini with Vegetables and Bacon

- 3 cups (600 g) rotini
- 2 tablespoons (30 ml) olive oil
- 1 shallot
- 2 garlic cloves
- 1 pound (.45 kg) asparagus, cut into 1" pieces
- 6 slices precooked bacon cut into 1" pieces
- 1 bell pepper cut into 1" pieces
- 1 cup (250 ml) chicken broth (made from a bouillon cube
- crumbled feta cheese
- pepper to taste

30 min

2 pots

DIFFICULTY

Easy

Serves 4

Cook the rotini in boiling water until half done, about ten minutes. Add the asparagus and bell pepper to the pot. Meanwhile, in a skillet, sauté the shallot and garlic in the oil until soft. Add the bacon. Add the chicken broth and heat. Drain the pasta and vegetables and add to the skillet. Add the crumbled feta cheese and stir gently until the cheese is mostly melted and the ingredients are combined. Season with pepper to taste.

Spaghetti

This simple recipe is easily adapted to serve more people and is a staple recipe for anyone camping in the wilderness.

- **reconstituted roll of dried spaghetti sauce (about 1 1/2 cups (350 ml)) or can of spaghetti sauce**
- **generous handful of spaghetti or other pasta**
- **1/4 cup (50 g) grated Parmesan or Romano cheese**

Cook pasta in boiling water until tender. Heat or reconstitute the sauce.

Pour the sauce over the pasta, sprinkle with Parmesan cheese and serve with garlic toast.

30 min

2 pots

DIFFICULTY

Easy

Serves 2

Variation:

Add sautéed mushrooms, onions, garlic, chopped pepperoni or other hard sausage.

If served early in a trip, sauté ground meat to mix with the sauce or, late in a trip, add reconstituted beef.

Ramen Noodles with Broccoli and Chicken

This is an easy dinner to make when the weather has turned against you.

- **package of ramen noodles**
- **can of chicken or tuna, drained**
- **broccoli, cut into small pieces**
- **slivered almonds**
- **egg**

Prepare the noodles according to the directions on the package. Cook for one or two minutes and then add the broccoli. Beat an egg and drizzle into the soup. Add the can of tuna or chicken. Add the slivered almonds. Stir in the packet of spices.

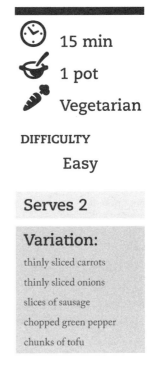

15 min

1 pot

Vegetarian

DIFFICULTY

Easy

Serves 2

Variation:

thinly sliced carrots

thinly sliced onions

slices of sausage

chopped green pepper

chunks of tofu

SANDWICHES

Lavosh

This is a fun, easy lunch to prepare. It's perfect early in the trip and is easily multiplied.

- **2 tortillas, 10 inches in diameter**
- **vacuum packed deli meats—ham, turkey or beef**
- **lettuce, chopped**
- **cream cheese—any flavor you desire**

Put a tortilla on a plate. Spread evenly with the cream cheese. Cover the tortilla with slices of meat, overlapping them. Leave about two inches uncovered along one edge. Spread the lettuce evenly over the meat, again leaving the same edge uncovered. This is so that the cream cheese will stick to the tortilla when you roll it up. Roll up the tortilla tightly toward the edge with only cream cheese on it. Press down and let sit for a minute so that the cream cheese sticks the roll together. Cut in half on the diagonal to serve in two pieces, or cut in small pieces, also on the diagonal, approximately 1 inch wide for a nice presentation. If you do this, just eat the ends before you serve the lavosh!

Serve with soup or cherry tomatoes and cucumber slices.

15 min

1 pot

DIFFICULTY

Easy

Pesto Foccacia Sandwich

- 1 round of foccacia bread, sliced in half crossways
- pesto sauce
- 1 finely sliced small–medium onion
- 1 medium tomato, sliced or cherry tomatoes, diced
- vacuum package of tuna or can, drained
- crumbled feta cheese (or grated or sliced other cheese)

Spread one side of the foccacia with the pesto sauce. Spread the onion, tomato and tuna evenly on top of the sauce. Add the cheese and top with the other piece of the foccacia to make a sandwich.

Add a little butter or ghee to a heated skillet. Cook the sandwich until lightly browned on one side. Turn over and cook on the other side. The cheese should be melting. Cut into quarters.

🕐 **15 min**

DIFFICULTY

Easy

Serves 4

Variation:

Use pita bread or English muffins to make individual sandwiches.

Quesadillas

'Queso' means 'cheese' in Spanish. This is an easy meal to prepare and other ingredients can be added for variation.

- 4, 8-inch tortillas
- 2 cups (400 g) Cheddar or Monterey Jack cheese, grated
- 1 teaspoon (3.5 ml) butter

Heat the skillet over medium heat. Add the butter. Place a tortilla in the pan, heat for a few seconds and turn over. Sprinkle the cheese evenly over the tortilla. Add other ingredients on top of the cheese to one half of the tortilla. Fold over the other half. The quesadilla now looks like an omelette. Turn the burner down and cook for a couple of minutes. Carefully turn over and cook on the other side until the cheese is melted. It should be lightly browned on both sides. Cut into three wedges.

Serve with a dollop of sour cream, salsa, guacamole or sliced avocado.

15 min

1 pot

DIFFICULTY

Easy

Serves 4

Options to add:

finely chopped mushrooms

finely chopped green onions

sliced black olives

chopped jalapeno peppers

vacuum pack of tuna or can of chicken

Easy Grilled Cheese Sandwiches

- **English muffins**
- sliced **Cheddar cheese, 1 slice per muffin**
- **butter**

Slice the muffins in half crosswise. Place the cheese on one half. Put the other half of the muffin on top. Butter one side of the muffin. Place on a heated skillet. Cook for a few minutes until slightly browned. Butter the other side. Turn over. Cook for a few minutes more until the cheese is melted.

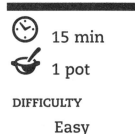

15 min

1 pot

DIFFICULTY

Easy

Serves 4

Variation:

Early in the trip, make with French or sourdough bread.

Add bacon bits or thin onion slices.

Serve with green pepper slices, cucumber slices and cherry tomatoes, sliced salami or pepperoni chunks.

Tuna Melt

- 1 tablespoon (15 ml) butter
- 4 thick slices of Italian bread or
  2 English muffins, cut in half
- vacuum package or can of tuna
- 1 tablespoon (15 ml) mayonnaise
- 1/2 teaspoon (5 ml) lemon juice
- 1/4 cup (50 g) finely chopped celery
- 1/4 cup (50 g) finely chopped green onions
- 2 teaspoons (20 ml) Worcestershire sauce
- 1 cup (200 g) grated cheese—
  Cheddar, Swiss or Gruyère

Melt the butter in a skillet. Fry the bread on both sides until toasted and golden. If using English muffins, toast on the cut side.

Combine the other ingredients, with the exception of the cheese, in a bowl. Divide and mound on the bread or muffins. Add the cheese on top. Place each piece back in the skillet on low heat. Cover and cook for a few minutes until the cheese is melted.

🕐 15 min

🥣 1 pot

DIFFICULTY

Easy

Serves 4

Variation:

Early in the trip, make with French or sourdough bread.

Add bacon bits or thin onion slices.

Serve with green pepper slices, cucumber slices and cherry tomatoes, sliced salami or pepperoni chunks.

English Muffins/Bagels with Lox and Cream Cheese

- 4 English muffins or bagels
- vacuum package of lox (cured salmon)
- capers
- thinly sliced red onion
- cream cheese

Slice the muffins in half crosswise. Spread cream cheese on each half. Add the lox, then the capers and onion.

Serve with sliced cucumber.

If bagels are being substituted for the English muffins, they need to be eaten very early in the trip. Despite being sturdy travelers, bagels become dry and hard after more than a couple of days.

🕑 15 min

DIFFICULTY
Easy

Serves 2

Variation:
Use pita bread or English muffins to make individual sandwiches.

Pita Pockets

Pita bread provides a great little pocket where you can insert all sorts of tasty ingredients for an easy lunch. Just put out the ingredients and let your fellow paddlers "do their own thing". The paddling chef can sit back and relax.

- **pita bread, sliced open sideways**
- **English cucumber, thinly sliced**
- **thin onion slices**
- **greens**
- **chopped cherry tomatoes**
- **vacuum packed or canned tuna or salmon**
- **diced left over cooked chicken or canned chicken**
- **diced ham, sausage**
- **grated Cheddar cheese**
- **tzatziki, mayonnaise, cream cheese, hummus**

Use any combination of the ingredients above to stuff the pita. Mix the chicken, tuna or salmon with the mayonnaise or tzatziki. Add greens, thin onion slices or other vegetables. Top with greens and cheese. Use your imagination and your favorite ingredients!

If using diced ham, consider mixing a little Dijon mustard or curry powder with mayonnaise.

If using sausage, consider mixing garlic powder or finely chopped garlic with the mayonnaise.

15 min

DIFFICULTY

Easy

Serves 4

Variation:

Use pita bread or English muffins to make individual sandwiches.

OUT OF THE SOIL

VEGETABLES & FRUITS

Many fruits and vegetables will travel well on paddling trips and provide an excellent source of vitamins, minerals and roughage. While some are fragile and need to be consumed at the beginning of a trip, they all need to be protected from bruising and cuts. Once damaged, unrefrigerated fruits and vegetables will rapidly deteriorate. Fragile fruits and vegetables packed in plastic containers need to breathe, so punch holes in the sides and line containers with a paper towel.

The recommendations that follow should be taken as a guide only. The daytime temperature on the trip will play a significant role in the longevity of your fruits and vegetables. I haven't included many recipes in this section, as there are easy recipes and combinations adaptable for paddling adventures. Most often, fresh fruits are just cut up and enjoyed and vegetables are either eaten raw or steamed. Look in your favorite cookbooks or troll the Internet. See the Dessert section for fruit recipes.

Fruits

Fragile Fruits (one or two days)

These fruits need to be well protected and consumed within the first one or two days. Berries are especially fragile. I don't recommend taking berries, with the possible exception of strawberries or blueberries, which are slightly hardier travelers than blackberries or raspberries. Really, don't consider taking blackberries or raspberries at all unless you're going to eat them on the first day. If you find berries growing in the wild, count yourself a lucky paddler, pick them and enjoy.

- berries
- peaches
- pears

Longer Lasting Fruits (three or four days)

These fruits also need to be protected while traveling.

- bananas
- nectarines
- kiwi fruit
- apricots
- grapes
- mangoes
- plums

Longest Lasting Fruits (up to a week or more)

These hardy fruits, with tougher skins, can be transported with ease. But still take care that they are not subjected to bruising, especially apples.

- apples
- oranges
- grapefruits
- pineapples
- lemons, limes (although they don't last as long as lemons because of their thinner skins)
- melons—depending on ripeness when starting out

I have found a wonderful new watermelon at our local grocery store. It's about the size of a cantaloupe, exceptionally sweet and seedless. Melons have to be eaten once cut open; they will not keep. Rinds are a garbage issue with most of these fruits, but fruit can really enhance the quality of meals on a longer paddling trip.

You'll want to decide in advance how much garbage you're willing to transport, or whether you may be able to make a fire to burn the vegetable and fruit waste.

Think about taking a little plastic container of lemon juice (available at most supermarkets) instead of fresh lemons, unless you have a meal plan that calls for lemon wedges. Lemon juice is handy for many recipes and you won't be left with the rinds to transport in your garbage bag. If lemon or lime zest is called for in a recipe, it can easily be dried at home.

Sliced fruit with yogurt is an easy dessert or breakfast, served with a toasted, buttered English muffin, bagel or crumpet.

Vegetables

Fragile Vegetables (two to three days)

As with the fragile fruits, these need to be well protected if taken on a paddling trip. Although fresh mushrooms and salad greens are included here, I've had both of these vegetables last for several days longer.

Buy plump, young mushrooms with no gills showing under the cap. Transport them in a paper bag inside a plastic container with holes punched in it to let the mushrooms breathe.

- asparagus spears
- tomatoes—except plum or "Roma" tomatoes which are intended to be cooked and will transport well if protected
- fresh mushrooms
- salad greens—in a resealable bag
- baby bok choi
- avocados—depending on ripeness when starting out
- endive

Longer Lasting Vegetables (three to six days)

These vegetables also need to be protected in transport—especially zucchini and eggplant, which have fragile skins.

- zucchini
- eggplant
- sweet peppers—green, yellow or red
- green beans
- snow peas
- green onions
- cherry or grape tomatoes (in a plastic container)
- broccoli
- cauliflower
- celery
- English cucumber (doesn't need to be peeled)
- leeks (cut off most of the green top and clean well at home)
- radicchio
- arugula
- escarole

Longest Lasting Vegetables

- carrots
- onions
- shallots
- potatoes
- garlic heads
- cabbage—green and red

VEGETABLES

Zucchini with Garlic

- 1 medium zucchini
- 1 tablespoon (15 ml) olive oil
- 1 clove garlic, finely chopped
- splash of lemon
- grated Parmesan cheese

Cut the zucchini into quarter-inch thick slices. Heat the oil in a skillet. Add the finely chopped garlic. Stir for a minute or two and add the zucchini. Sauté for a few minutes until the zucchini is slightly browned. Turn the zucchini slices and cook until the second side is slightly browned. Drizzle with a splash of lemon juice and sprinkle with Parmesan cheese.

15 min

1 pot

Vegetarian

DIFFICULTY

Easy

Serves 2

Ratatouille

- 1 onion, cut into one-inch pieces
- 1 eggplant, thickly sliced and cut in pieces
- 1 zucchini, thickly sliced and cut in pieces
- 2 medium tomatoes, chopped into one inch pieces
- olive oil
- 1/2 cup (100 g) grated Parmesan or Romano cheese
- salt and pepper to taste

In a skillet, sauté the onion for one or two minutes. Add the eggplant and zucchini. Cook for a few minutes more. Add the tomatoes. Continue cooking until all the vegetables are softened. Add grated Parmesan cheese and stir to combine. The cheese will melt into the vegetable mixture. Season with salt and pepper.

15 min

1 pot

Vegetarian

DIFFICULTY

Easy

Serves 4 to 6

Green Cabbage with Garlic

- **One-half head green cabbage, thinly sliced**
- **2 garlic cloves, finely chopped**
- **1/4 to 1/2 cup (60 to 125 ml) water**
- **knob of butter or vegetable oil**
- **pepper**

Pour the water into the skillet and heat until simmering. Add the cabbage. Cook the cabbage over the lowest heat, stirring frequently, until all of the water is absorbed, 15 minutes or so. Add more water if necessary. The cabbage should be softened. Add the butter and continue to stir. Add the garlic and stir until the garlic is cooked. Season to taste with pepper.

🕐 30 min

1 pot

🥕 Vegetarian

DIFFICULTY

Easy

Serves 4

Seared Asparagus

- **1 pound (450 g) asparagus spears**
- **1 tablespoon (15 ml) lemon juice**
- **1/4 cup (60 ml) butter or vegetable oil**
- **salt and pepper, to taste**

Heat the skillet over the burner. Add the butter and heat until bubbly. Add the asparagus in a single layer. Shake the pan to rotate the asparagus as it becomes charred in spots. Sprinkle with the lemon juice and add salt and pepper to taste.

Serve with fresh caught fish early in the trip.

🕐 15 min

1 pot

🥕 Vegetarian

DIFFICULTY

Easy

Serves 4

Variation:

Top with a poached egg and crumbled feta cheese for a light dinner. Serve with cherry tomatoes and garlic toast or pasta.

Combine one-quarter cup (50g) finely chopped almonds with one-quarter cup (50 g) grated Parmesan cheese (can be taken in a zip lock bag). Sprinkle on top of the hot asparagus when serving.

Glazed Carrots

- 2 tablespoons (30 ml) butter or vegetable oil
- 1/4 cup (50 g) brown sugar
- 2 tablespoons (30 ml) Dijon mustard
- 2 1/2 to 3 cups (500 g to 600 g) carrots, sliced diagonally, or the equivalent amount of pre-packaged baby carrots

Cook the carrots in boiling water until just tender. Do not overcook. Drain.

Combine the butter, brown sugar and mustard in a cup. Add to the pot with the carrots. Return to the heat and stir gently until the carrots are evenly glazed.

15 min

1 pot

Vegetarian

DIFFICULTY

Easy

Serves 4 to 6

Variation:

Add sliced green pepper when the carrots are about half cooked.

Green Beans with Slivered Almonds

- 1/2 pound (275 g) green beans, trimmed and left whole or cut in half
- 1 clove garlic, finely chopped
- 2 tablespoons (30 ml) butter or vegetable oil
- 1/4 cup (50 g) slivered almonds
- freshly grated pepper

Cook the green beans in a pot with a little water until done, but still crisp. Drain. Remove from the pot and keep warm. Melt the butter in the pot and sauté the garlic. Add the slivered almonds. Cook until the almonds are browning. Return the beans to the pot and toss to combine. Add the grated pepper.

15 min

1 pot

Vegetarian

DIFFICULTY

Easy

Serves 2

Variation:

Take a can of green beans or dehydrated beans for late in a trip.

Substitute bacon bits or chopped, precooked bacon for the almonds.

Leeks with Parmesan Cheese

At home: Leeks need to be cleaned well of any sand or soil. Cut off most of the green top. Pat dry for transport wrapped in a paper towel.

- **2 leeks cut in quarter-inch thick slices**
- **2 tablespoons (30 ml) butter**
- **1/4 cup (60 ml) water**

SAUCE:
- **2 teaspoons (10 g) flour**
- **1/2 cup (125 ml) milk**

Mix the flour and milk in a cup until smooth.

TOPPING:
- **1/4 cup (50 g) grated Parmesan cheese**
- **freshly grated pepper**

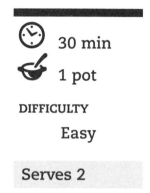

30 min

1 pot

DIFFICULTY

Easy

Serves 2

Sauté the leeks in a skillet with the butter for a few minutes, until lightly browned. Add the water. Cover and simmer for several more minutes, lifting the lid to stir while cooking. Remove the lid and add the sauce to the leeks and stir until smooth. Stir until the sauce is cooked and has thickened. Add a little water or white wine if the sauce becomes too thick. Sprinkle with the Parmesan cheese and grated pepper, and serve.

This is an excellent accompaniment to pork tenderloin or ham. Romano or Asiago cheese can be substituted for the Parmesan.

Baby Bok Choi

- 2 tablespoons (30 ml) butter or vegetable oil
- 4 garlic cloves, minced
- 6 to 8 baby bok choi (depending on size)
- 1 cup (250 ml) chicken or vegetable broth

In a small skillet, sauté the garlic in melted butter or oil. Add the bok choi and sauté until slightly charred. Add the broth. Simmer until the bok choi is cooked through, a few minutes.

15 min

1 pot

Vegetarian

DIFFICULTY

Easy

Serves 4

Braised Belgian Endive with Garlic

- 4 heads endive
- 4 tablespoons (60 ml) olive oil
- 2 cloves garlic, finely chopped
- 1 teaspoon (5 g) dried basil

Heat the oil in a skillet. Place the endive beside each other in the skillet. Sprinkle with the garlic and basil. Cook over low heat for 10 to 15 minutes until tender, shaking the pan to rotate the endive to cook evenly.

Serve with a fresh meat meal early in the trip, or with fresh-caught fish.

15 min

1 pot

Vegetarian

DIFFICULTY

Easy

Serves 4

POTATOES

Garlic Potatoes

This is an adaptation of a recipe that Leslie's brother-in-law Paul Churchland makes. This internationally respected philosopher is also a genial host and a great cook.

- 10 to 12 small new potatoes
- olive oil
- 3 minced garlic cloves, or 1 teaspoon (5 g) powdered garlic
- 1 teaspoon (5g) Cavender's All Purpose Greek Seasoning

Cut the potatoes in half. Boil until almost cooked. Drain the water. Toss the potatoes with enough olive oil to coat. Add the garlic and seasoning. Return to the heat and sauté, stirring often, for a few minutes until lightly browned and cooked through.

15 min

1 pot

Vegetarian

DIFFICULTY

Easy

Serves 4

Dijon Mustard Potatoes

This dish is an excellent accompaniment to fried ham or filet of beef.

- 4 Yukon Gold potatoes (or other that don't need peeling)
- 2 tablespoons (30 ml) Dijon mustard
- 1/2 cup (125 ml) milk or sour cream
- salt and pepper to taste

Cut the potatoes into pieces and boil until cooked through. Drain. Mash with a fork. Add the mustard and milk or sour cream. Mash well to combine. Add salt and pepper to taste.

Replace the dairy product with vegetable broth to make this dish vegan.

15 min

1 pot

Vegetarian

DIFFICULTY

Easy

Serves 4

Potato Patties

These easy-to-make potato patties make a great snack or can accompany a meal as the carbohydrate component in place of rice or pasta.

- **4 Yukon Gold potatoes**
- **3 tablespoons (45 g) corn flour or plain flour**
- **dash of salt**
- **oil or ghee**

Cut the potatoes into pieces and cook in a pot of boiling water. Drain the potatoes. Mash with a fork. Add the flour and salt. Mix well. The mixture should become like a dough and not crumble.

Roll a large golf-ball sized piece of the potato mixture in your hand. Flatten it in your palm.

Fry the patties for a few minutes in an oiled skillet over medium heat until golden brown on both sides. Ghee works well for this recipe.

Serve with chutney or vinegar as a snack, or as a carb with dinner.

30 min

2 pots

Vegetarian

DIFFICULTY

Easy

Serves 4

Gnocchi

Think of these tiny potato dumplings much like pasta, and serve them with a variety of sauces. Cheese sauce is especially good. Gnocchi is a nice accompaniment to fresh meat or ham.

• 1 1/2 cups (300 g) gnocchi

Boil approximately 4 cups of water in a pot, adding a little salt. Cook the gnocchi in batches, removing them after they have risen to the surface. Place in a bowl and cover.

Toss with:
- Pesto sauce and Parmesan
- Olive oil or butter
- Parmesan or Asiago cheese
- Tomato sauce
- Bacon bits

15 min

1 pot

Vegetarian

DIFFICULTY

Easy

Serves 4

BEANS & PEAS

Tipsy Beans with Sausage

- 4 tablespoons (60 ml) olive oil
- 3 or 4 chorizo sausages, sliced
- 4 jalapeno peppers, whole
- 1 onion, finely chopped
- 4 tomatoes, chipped
- 1, 14 ounce (398 ml) can pinto beans, drained
- pepper, to taste
- 1 can beer
- 1/2 cup (100g) freeze-dried cilantro

🕐 30 min

🥣 1 pot

DIFFICULTY

Easy

Serves 4

Heat the oil in a skillet over medium heat. Add the sausages and peppers and fry until brown. Add the onion and tomatoes. Stir in the beans, cilantro, pepper and beer. Turn down the heat and simmer for 15 minutes or so until thickened.

Serve with tortillas or over rice.

Kidney Beans with Yogurt

This is another easy meal to prepare when your camp is being drenched with liquid sunshine.

- 2 tablespoons (30 ml) butter or olive oil
- 2 tablespoons (20 g) curry powder
- 2 garlic cloves, finely chopped
- 1 tablespoon (15 ml) lemon juice or juice of 1 lemon
- 1/2 onion, chopped
- 1, 14 ounce (398 ml) can kidney beans, drained
- 3 tablespoons (45 ml) yogurt
- 1/2 teaspoon (2.5 ml) dried thyme
- 2 green onions, chopped

In a skillet over medium heat, add the butter or oil. Add the onions and curry powder. Sauté for a few minutes until the onion is softened. Add the remaining ingredients and simmer gently until heated through.

Serve over rice and sprinkle with the green onion.

15 min

1 pot

Vegetarian

DIFFICULTY

Easy

Serves 2

Chili

This hearty, popular meal is also one that can be modified by adding a variety of other ingredients to create an easy one-pot dish. It is quite possible to make chili from scratch on a paddling trip, but it's time-consuming and would use a good deal of fuel. But if you want to soak the beans for the day as you paddle and can take turns stirring the pot over an open fire, by all means, go for it. I haven't included a recipe for homemade chili. I use either dried chili mix, found in bulk food stores, reconstituted dried chili made at home, or a can of chili.

One can, or its dried equivalent, will feed two people with your own additions.

Heat the chili in a pot and add whatever additions you like. Stir to combine until heated through.

🕐 **15 min**

🥣 **1 pot**

🥕 **Vegetarian**

DIFFICULTY

Easy

Serves 2

POSSIBLE ADDITIONS:
- **chunks of sausage, bacon or ham**
- **reconstituted hamburger or buffalo burger**
- **reconstituted pinto beans or can of pinto beans**
- **reconstituted crushed tomatoes or can of tomatoes, coarsely chopped**
- **reconstituted dried corn or small can of corn**
- **chopped onion**
- **chopped green pepper**
- **Tabasco sauce or dried chili flakes, for a kick**

Serve with cheese biscuits or garlic toast and cucumber or green pepper slices

Spiced Garbanzo Beans

Serve as an appetizer for four, or as an accompaniment to a meal for two or three. Make it on a leisurely day. It needs to stand for an hour for the flavors to mingle, but doesn't require any cooking. Read a book or write your journal while you wait.

60 min

Vegetarian

DIFFICULTY

Easy

Serves 2 to 4

* 1 can garbanzo beans (chick peas)
* 1 teaspoon (5 g) amchur (mango) powder
* 1 teaspoon (5 g) masala (curry) powder
* juice of one lemon
* salt, to taste
* 1 medium sweet onion, thinly sliced
* 1 tablespoon (15 g) freeze-dried coriander leaves
* 2 green chilies, sliced thinly, lengthwise

Drain the water from the garbanzo beans. Combine the next four ingredients in a small bowl. Combine with the garbanzo beans. Add the chilies, onions and the coriander. Toss to combine. Let stand for 1 hour.

Peanuts with Zesty Masala

Made at home and taken in an airtight container, this is a tasty snack eaten either on or off the water. Imagine yourself in your canoe, leisurely trolling for lake trout, nibbling these spicy peanuts.

- 1 cup (200 g) roasted peanuts
- 1/2 cup (100 g) gram (chick pea) flour
- 1/4 cup (50 g) rice flour
- 1 1/2 teaspoons (8 g) chili powder
- 1/4 teaspoon (dash) salt
- water
- oil or ghee

Combine the dry ingredients in a bowl. Stir in the peanuts and add four or five tablespoons of water. Stir until the peanuts are well coated.

Heat the oil in a wok or deep skillet. Drop the peanuts into the hot oil. Separate the peanuts as they cook. Continue to cook over medium heat until the peanuts are golden brown.

Cool. Place in an airtight container for transport.

15 min

Vegetarian

DIFFICULTY

Easy

Serves 2 to 4

TOFU

This soy product is an excellent source of protein for paddlers who are vegetarians or who wish to enhance their meals with a variation on animal based proteins. Firm tofu is a good product to take on a paddling trip, as it can be stir fried, grilled or added to soup dishes. It can also be pre-cooked or dehydrated. Aseptic cardboard containers, which need no refrigeration prior to being opened are ideal, but vacuum packages of firm tofu travel well. Tofu will also freeze well, can be transported frozen, like meats, and will keep for a couple of days.

Teriyaki Tofu with Vegetables

- 12 ounces (375 g) firm tofu cut into small cubes
- 1/3 cup (75 ml) teriyaki sauce
- 2 tablespoons (30 ml) butter or olive oil
- 4 baby bok choi, cut in half lengthwise
- 1 cup (250 g) baby carrots, sliced in half lengthwise
- 1 sweet red onion, coarsely chopped
- 1/4 cup (60 ml) white wine
- sesame seeds or pine nuts to garnish

60 min

1 pot

Vegetarian

DIFFICULTY

Moderate

Serves 4

Marinate the tofu in the teriyaki sauce for half an hour.

Heat the butter or oil in a skillet. Reserve the marinade and fry the tofu for 2 to 3 minutes on each side until golden. Remove the tofu from the pan and keep warm. Add more oil to the pan and sauté the onion for a few minutes. Add the carrots and cook for a few minutes more. Then add the bok choi. Add the wine, the reserved marinade and the tofu to the skillet. Stir for a minute or two until the flavors are combined. Sprinkle the servings with sesame seeds or pine nuts.

Portobello Mushrooms Stuffed with Tofu

- **4 Portobello mushrooms—
  remove the stalks and chop finely**
- **12 ounces (375 g) firm tofu,
  cut into small pieces**
- **1/2 cup (125 g) green onions, finely chopped**
- **2 cloves garlic, finely chopped**
- **1/3 cup (200 g) corn niblets, fresh,
  or dried and reconstituted**
- **1/3 cup (75 ml) soy sauce**
- **1/4 teaspoon (pinch) chili pepper**
- **3 tablespoons (50 ml) sesame oil or olive oil**

60 min

2 pots

Vegetarian

DIFFICULTY

Moderate

Serves 4

At home, combine the soy sauce and chili pepper in a small container. In camp, add the tofu. Marinate for half an hour.

Heat the oil in a skillet. Sauté the chopped mushroom stalks, green onions and garlic. Add the corn. Add the tofu and the marinade. Cook for a few minutes until the mixture is heated through and the vegetables are softened.

Divide the tofu/vegetable mixture between the four mushroom caps. Place them on a skillet with a little oil. Cover and cook over medium heat for ten minutes or so, until the mushrooms are heated through and softened.

Tofu with Sweet and Sour Sauce

- 1 pound (454 g) firm tofu
- 4 tablespoons (60 ml) soy sauce
- 2 tablespoons (30 ml) sesame oil
- 2 tablespoons (30 ml) sesame seeds
- 1/2 onion, finely chopped

SAUCE:
- 1 tablespoon (15 ml) soy sauce
- 1 teaspoon (5 ml) sesame oil
- 1 tablespoon (15 ml) vinegar
- 1 tablespoon (15 ml) honey

30 min

1 pot

Vegetarian

DIFFICULTY

Easy

Serves 4

At home, combine the ingredients for the sauce in a small, sealed container.

Cube the tofu. In a skillet, heat the oil. Add the onions and the tofu. Fry for several minutes, stirring so that the tofu is golden and the onion softened. Remove from the heat and toss with the sauce.

Serve with stir-fried vegetables or a salad.

SALADS

Potato Salad

- **4 or 5 small new potatoes**
- **mayonnaise**
- **1 or 2 hard boiled eggs**
- **1/4 cup (50 g) finely chopped onion or green onion**
- **salt and pepper to taste**

Ever thinking ahead, you will have cooked more potatoes than needed for dinner the previous night. Cool them and store in a zip lock bag. In the morning, while making breakfast, hard boil one or two eggs. Keep cool. At lunch, cut the potatoes into small pieces and chop the eggs. Combine with the finely chopped onion and enough mayonnaise to moisten.

30 min

1 pot

DIFFICULTY

Easy

Serves 2

Variation:

add finely chopped green pepper or celery

add 1 teaspoon (5 ml) Dijon mustard

Bocconcini and Tomato Salad

- 2 bocconcini (marinated, unripened mozzarella cheese) in a container with a little oil
- 2 large tomatoes
- herbed Italian salad dressing

Slice the bocconcini and the tomatoes into slices about a quarter of an inch thick. Place on plates, alternating the cheese and tomato slices. Drizzle with the dressing.

Accompany with chunks of Italian bread and sausage for lunch early in the trip.

15 min

Vegetarian

DIFFICULTY

Easy

Serves 4

Variation:

Use approximately 24 baby bocconcini (available at some Italian markets) and cherry tomatoes instead of the baseball sized versions of same.

Hearty Salad

- 1 endive, coarsely chopped
- one-half a romaine lettuce, coarsely chopped
- small bunch of escarole, coarsely chopped
- one-half a head of radicchio, coarsely chopped
- 1 cup (200 g) crumbled feta cheese
- 1/2 cup (100 g) coarsely chopped walnuts
- vinaigrette
- 1/2 cup (125 ml) olive oil
- 2 tablespoons (30 ml) balsamic vinegar

Put the salad ingredients in a bowl. Combine the oil and vinegar in a cup or transport in a small container. Drizzle over the salad and toss to combine.

15 min

Vegetarian

DIFFICULTY

Easy

Serves 4 to 6

Variation:

Add chunks of pepperoni, chicken or chopped ham to make a meal for lunch or an easy dinner.

Green Salad with Salmon

- salad greens
- cherry tomatoes, sliced in half
- can or vacuum package of salmon
- pine nuts
- Italian salad dressing or oil and vinegar
- pepper to taste

Toss the salad ingredients together with the dressing. Arrange on two plates. Add the salmon and sprinkle the pine nuts on top of the salad.

Serve with Cheesy Pita Bread page 75.

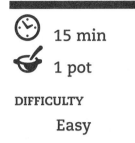

15 min

1 pot

DIFFICULTY

Easy

Serves 2

Greek Salad

- half an English cucumber chopped into half-inch pieces
- half a medium sweet red onion, coarsely chopped
- 1 green pepper, coarsely chopped
- 3/4 cup (150 g) crumbled feta cheese
- 1/2 cup (100 g) sliced black olives
- 2 coarsely chopped medium tomatoes or a handful of cherry tomatoes, halved
- 1/2 cup (125 ml) oil and vinegar or herbed salad dressing

Toss all the ingredients in a bowl and serve as a side dish.

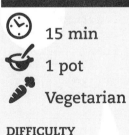

15 min

1 pot

Vegetarian

DIFFICULTY

Easy

Serves 4 to 6

Salad Niçoise with Pasta

This is an elegant lunch if you are at an excellent camp for two or three days, enjoying beautiful summer weather.

- 3 cups (600 g) rotini or other curly pasta
- 1/2 pound (.25 kg) fresh green beans, trimmed
- 2 medium tomatoes, cut into wedges
- 1 red onion, sliced thinly
- 1/2 cup (100 g) pitted black olives
- 2 hard boiled eggs, shelled, cut into 6 wedges each
- small jar of marinated artichokes, cut into quarters
- vacuum package of tuna or small can, drained
- prepared Italian dressing or oil and vinegar

30 min

1 pot

DIFFICULTY

Moderate

Serves 6 for lunch or 4 for a light dinner

Hard boil the eggs in a pot of boiling water. Remove from the pot with a spoon, set aside and cool. (Or, if in camp for the day, cook the eggs at breakfast and set aside until lunch). Add the pasta to the boiling water. When almost done, add the green beans. When the beans are cooked but still crisp, remove them from the pot and set aside. Continue cooking the pasta until done. Drain the pasta. Stir with a little oil so the pasta doesn't stick together. Let cool. In a bowl, combine the pasta, the beans, tomatoes, artichokes, onion and tuna. Toss with the dressing.

Arrange the salad on plates and garnish with the eggs.

Caesar Salad

- 1 head romaine lettuce
- croutons—commercially made, transported in a zip lock bag, or made from left over baguette at camp
- package of Caesar salad dressing
- grated Parmesan or Romano cheese

Prepare the dressing according to the package directions.

If making the croutons from last evening's left over baguette, cut the baguette into half-inch cubes. Melt a little butter in a skillet. Add the pieces of bread and sauté, tossing to brown on all sides. Sprinkle with a little oregano if desired.

Coarsely chop the lettuce. Toss with the dressing and croutons. Sprinkle with the cheese.

15 min

1 pot

DIFFICULTY

Easy

Serves 4 to 6

Tuna Salad with Avocado

- salad greens
- 1 avocado, halved and sliced
- cherry tomatoes, sliced in half
- thin slices of sweet red onion,
  or chopped green onion
- 1 can tuna or vacuum package
- capers
- ground pepper
- oil and vinegar dressing, with herbs, if desired
- hard boiled egg, quartered

🕐 **15 min**

DIFFICULTY

Easy

Serves 2

Variation:

On the first day of the trip, cook a boneless, skinless chicken breast to substitute for the tuna. Slice and serve on top of the other salad ingredients for a warm dinner.

Arrange the salad greens on two plates. Add the avocado, tomatoes and onion to make a nice presentation. Top with the flaked tuna and sprinkle with the capers. Grind a little pepper on top and drizzle with the dressing. Garnish with the hard boiled egg.

This salad will also work as a light dinner, served on a warm summer's evening, accompanied by any of the easy breads; garlic toast, naan, pita or English muffins.

Rotini with Pesto and Cherry Tomato Salad

This is an easy recipe to serve for lunch. It can also be prepared at home and transported in a plastic container for lunch or as an accompaniment to dinner for the first day of a trip.

- 1 1/2 cups (300g) dried rotini
- 1 tablespoon (15 ml) olive oil
- 1/2 cup (125 ml) pesto sauce
- 4 or 5 cherry tomatoes, cut in half
- 1/4 cup (50 g) pine nuts
- 1/4 cup (50 g) grated Parmesan cheese

Cook the rotini in a pot of boiling water until al dente. Drain the pot. Add a tablespoon of olive oil to the pasta and stir so the pasta will not stick together. Let cool. Stir in the pesto sauce, pine nuts and cherry tomatoes.

Serve on individual plates and sprinkle with the Parmesan cheese.

30 min

1 pot

Vegetarian

DIFFICULTY

Easy

Serves 4

Variation:

Flake a vacuum package of tuna or can of chicken. Add to the pasta before sprinkling the Parmesan.

Add a small jar of drained, chopped artichoke hearts or slices of green pepper.

Raita—Indian Cucumber Salad

This is an adaptation of a most popular Indian recipe and can be served as a healthy accompaniment to a number of recipes in this book. As it is a salad, it requires no cooking.

- 1 English cucumber, sliced thinly
- 1 cup (250 g) yogurt
- 2 green onions, sliced thinly
- 1/4 teaspoon (pinch) cayenne or red chili powder
- 1 tablespoon (15 ml) lemon juice

Combine all the ingredients in a bowl. Let sit for a few minutes to let the flavors combine.

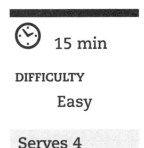 15 min

DIFFICULTY

Easy

Serves 4

Moo and Cluck

DAIRY PRODUCTS & EGGS

Eggs, cheese and other milk products such as yogurt, sour cream and cream cheese are excellent accompaniments on paddling trips and can be used in many recipes. When any milk product is spoiling, it gives off a clearly identifiable sour odor. If cheese has mould, it should not be eaten.

Eggs

Fresh eggs will easily last for a week or more. I have transported them successfully on many journeys in a plastic egg container, not withstanding my disaster in Gwaii Haanas Park.

Mayonnaise

A small jar of mayonnaise will keep for up to a week in moderate temperatures, less than 80° F. (27° C) during the day, cooler at night.

Milk

Fresh milk is not reasonably taken on any paddling trip. However, dried milk is a most useful component of the food stores. Dried milk can be added to other dry ingredients when preparing zip lock bags at home. Just remember to add the appropriate amount of water at camp. Otherwise, take the dried milk in a separate zip lock bag, prepare the appropriate amount at camp and add it to the recipe you have in mind. All of the recipes in this book assume that you understand these two possibilities.

Yogurt and Sour Cream

Yogurt and sour cream can be carried for up to a week. Plain yogurt can be used in a variety of recipes. A lovely fruit salad can be made from apple and melon slices, grapes and yogurt sprinkled with chopped walnuts. Sour cream is a tasty addition to potato dishes, tacos or quesadillas.

Cream Cheese

Cream cheese comes in different flavors and can be spread on crackers for a simple pre-dinner snack, or incorporated into other recipes. Like yogurt and sour cream, it will keep up to a week in moderate temperatures.

Butter and Oil

Butter keeps well on a paddling trip. I've had butter in a plastic container soften on a hot summer's day only to harden again overnight when hung over the branch of a tree in a dry bag. A small bottle of olive oil can be used in combination with vinegar and herbs to make salad dressing or to sauté meats or vegetables. I don't recommend margarine. Ghee, page 157, is an excellent product to substitute for ordinary butter but requires some time and effort at home to prepare.

Cheese

What a wonderful food to take on a paddling trip! There are so many kinds of cheese that can be taken successfully and incorporated into recipes. Leslie and I have regularly rewarded ourselves at the end of a paddling day with Camembert cheese and crackers accompanied by a glass of wine while preparing dinner. Ask at your favorite deli counter about well-flavored cheeses that will travel. After all, most cheeses were created when refrigeration did not exist.

Camembert or Brie in sealed tins from the manufacturer, don't need refrigeration and will keep for the duration of your trip. We were still enjoying crackers with Camembert on the last evenings when we were in Gwaii Haanas Park.

Hard cheeses such as Cheddar, Parmesan, Romano and provolone, wrapped in tin foil, will keep for a week or more. Cut the cheese into small blocks about three or four inches square. Wrap tightly in tin foil.

Feta can be taken dry or in the brine that's sometimes included with the cheese. Dry feta is more easily transported, as you don't have the liquid to contend with. I've had a dry pack of feta keep happily for more than a week.

Marinated bocconcini, transported in a sealed plastic container, is a wonderful treat, served early in the trip accompanied by tomatoes as a salad with a vinaigrette dressing.

Many of the recipes in this book include cheese as an ingredient, but I've included a few recipes that focus on cheese in this chapter.

A Big Egg Crash

Isle 225, Gwaii Haanas Park
July, 2002

Paddling around the little peninsula into Jedway, we can see remains of the cannery from the water. The area is blanketed with moss and foxgloves are blooming in the grassy glade. A black-tailed deer wanders through, unconcerned by our presence.

Our excitement grows: remnants from the cannery days are scattered about. While they're described by some writers as industrial trash, Leslie and I see them as reminders of the history here. Remains of Haida town sites are rightly revered as great pieces of cultural history but I place no less importance in the more recent history of the Japanese, Chinese and European miners; fishermen, and cannery workers who traveled thousands of miles from their birthplaces, dreaming of a better life. An old iron stove, bricks, an old boot and shards of the familiar blue and white china commonly used by the Japanese paint a picture of life here. Curiously, several large rocks on the shore have been modified with a dash of concrete, creating a flat seat. Shells, or in one case, a small pottery bowl, have been embedded in the same rock. Our most haunting find is the top portion of a woman's lace-up boot. The leather is fine and the circumference indicates a small, delicate foot wore this shoe.

The branch we chose to hang our food on last night broke while we were hauling up the dry bags and I discovered, to my great disappointment, that all of our remaining eggs were broken. The tasty omelette served for dinner last evening will be, it turns out, our only one of the trip. We have always carried eggs successfully in a plastic container expressly meant for this purpose but I have, in the past, stored them flat on the top of a dry bag. This time, they were on their side in the bottom, to make for efficient packing and so took the full brunt when the bag fell. My dinner and breakfast plans for the rest of the trip have to undergo some serious modifications.

Fried Eggs and Ham with Hollandaise Sauce

- 2 English muffins, cut in half and buttered
- 4 eggs
- 4 slices of ham
- a little butter or oil
- package of Hollandaise sauce

Prepare the Hollandaise sauce according to package directions in a small pot. Set aside. Heat the butter or oil in a skillet. Fry the eggs and the slices of ham. Put the eggs on top of the ham slices and move them to the side of the skillet. Place the English muffins on the skillet buttered side down and heat until slightly browned. Return the Hollandaise sauce to the burner to reheat.

Put the muffins on plates, top with the ham and eggs and finish with the Hollandaise sauce.

Serve with orange slices for breakfast or vegetables for dinner.

🕐 30 min

🥣 2 pots

DIFFICULTY

Moderate

Serves 2

This recipe can serve four people with smaller appetites.

Variation:

add sautéed mushrooms

poach the eggs instead of frying

add sautéed chopped green peppers or onions

Omelette

- **4 eggs, beaten**
- **a little water**
- **butter or oil for the pan**

Beat the eggs together with a fork or small whisk until well combined. Add the water and stir. Heat the oil or butter in the skillet. Pour the eggs into the skillet. Add any other ingredients that appeal to you.

Additions: sautéed mushrooms, onions, grated cheese, chopped sausage, green peppers, tomatoes or herbs

15 min

1 pot

Vegetarian

DIFFICULTY

Easy

Serves 2

French Toast

This is a good way to use up the leftover baguette from the first night's dinner.

- **6 slices of a baguette, 1 inch thick**
- **2 eggs, mixed with 2 tablespoons (30 ml) water**
- **butter**
- **cinnamon**
- **maple syrup**

Mix the egg and water in a shallow plate. Soak the slices of bread on both sides in the egg mixture. Sauté in a buttered skillet for a few minutes, or until the bread is lightly browned. Turn. Sprinkle the top side with cinnamon. Serve with maple syrup.

Serving suggestions:

- sliced oranges
- sliced apples
- sausages
- fresh berries, gathered at camp

15 min

1 pot

Vegetarian

DIFFICULTY

Easy

Serves 2

Variation:

For a savory French toast, use only the first three ingredients. Serve with sautéed mushrooms and top with grated cheese or diced ham. I confess to liking ketchup with savory French toast.

Salmon Frittata with Onions, Mushrooms and Green Pepper

The possibilities for a frittata are only limited by the available ingredients and the chef's imagination. Here's just a sample recipe.

- **6 eggs**
- **2-3 tablespoons (30-45 ml) water**
- **dash of salt and pepper**
- **vacuum pack or can of salmon**
- **1/2 cup (100 g) chopped onions**
- **1/2 cup (100 g) chopped mushrooms**
- **1/2 cup (100 g) chopped green pepper**
- **1/2 cup (100 g) grated Cheddar cheese**
- **oil or butter**

Beat the eggs in a bowl with the water. Add salt and pepper.

Sauté the vegetables in a skillet with a little oil or butter. Remove from the pan. Pour the egg mixture into the pan. Spread the vegetables and the salmon evenly over the eggs. Sprinkle the grated Cheddar evenly over the mixture. Cover and cook until the egg is firm and the cheese is melted.

Cut into pie-shaped pieces to serve.

30 min

1 pot

DIFFICULTY

Moderate

Serves 2

Variation:

Use any combination of vegetables you like including garlic, sun-dried tomatoes, capers, broccoli, left over cooked potatoes.

Use other cheeses—Asiago, feta, Parmesan.

Add interesting herbs or dried chili pepper flakes.

Add diced sausage, a can of chicken, or tuna.

Breakfast Burritos

This recipe is a great way to use up bits and pieces of left over vegetables, and is easily modified to serve more paddlers.

- 4 eggs
- **butter or vegetable oil for the pan**
- **two small tortillas**

Heat the butter or oil in the pan. Start with any ingredients you want to add to the burrito; finely chopped mushrooms, onions, green pepper, etc. Sauté until cooked. Add the eggs and stir the combination to make scrambled eggs. Put an equal measure into the middle of the tortillas, tuck in the ends, and roll up.

Serve with salsa on the side or put a few drops of Tabasco sauce in the egg mixture for a little kick.

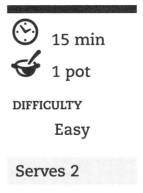

15 min

1 pot

DIFFICULTY

Easy

Serves 2

Egg Drop Soup

This is a simple, versatile recipe, and other ingredients can be added to make a light meal. Think of adding any vegetables you have on hand, including diced ham or chicken.

- **4 cups (1 liter) chicken broth**
- **2 eggs, lightly beaten**
- **freshly grated pepper**
- **1/2 cup (100 g) green onions, finely chopped**

Heat the broth in a pot and bring to a boil. Add the pepper. Turn down the heat on the burner. Slowly pour the eggs into the broth, stirring until the eggs are cooked and form threads in the broth.

Garnish with the green onions and serve.

15 min

1 pot

DIFFICULTY

Easy

Serves 4

Cheese Fondue

- 1/2 cup (125 g) Gruyère cheese
- 1 cup (250 g) Emmentaler or Swiss cheese
- 1 garlic clove, finely chopped
- 1 cup (250 ml) dry white wine
- 1 tablespoon (15 ml) kirsch (optional) or
  1 tablespoon (15 ml) lemon juice
- 1 tablespoon (15 g) cornstarch
- baguette cut into 1 inch cubes, preferably a
  day-old loaf.

30 min

1 pot

DIFFICULTY

Easy

Serves 4

Cut the cheese into small cubes. Reserve a little of the wine and combine with the cornstarch and the kirsch or the lemon juice. Stir together the cheese, the garlic and the rest of the wine in a pot over low heat. Stirring constantly, bring just to a boil. Add the cornstarch mixture. Continue stirring for a short time, until the fondue is smooth.

Skewer the bread on forks or sticks and coat with the cheese. Accompany with a salad.

If you drop a piece of bread into the fondue, tradition has it that you have to kiss all the members of the opposite sex.

At the end of the meal, divide the crusty bits of cheese that have stuck on the bottom of the pot amongst the members of the group. This is the prize.

Cheese Tortellini Salad with Chicken and Vegetables

- 8 ounces (225 g) cheese-stuffed tortellini
- 1 can of chicken, flaked
- 1/4 cup (50 g) cherry tomatoes, quartered
- 3/4 cup (150 g) broccoli florets
- 3/4 cup (150 g) crumbled feta cheese
- oil and vinegar, or herbed Italian dressing

Cook the tortellini in a pot of boiling water until almost done. Add the broccoli florets. Continue cooking until the pasta is cooked al dente (cooked, but with a little bite) and the broccoli still retains a little crunch. Drain and let cool. Add the tomatoes, chicken and the cheese. Toss with the dressing.

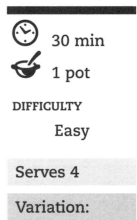

30 min

1 pot

DIFFICULTY

Easy

Serves 4

Variation:

Add the tomatoes, chicken and cheese to the pasta while still hot for a light dinner.

Serve with a salad.

Crêpes with Tuna in Mushroom Cream Sauce with Sun-Dried Tomatoes

- **Crêpe batter recipe page 72**
- **Package mushroom cream sauce or Alfredo sauce**
- **3/4 cup (150 g) mushrooms, chopped**
- **1 garlic clove, finely chopped**
- **4 to 6 pieces of sun-dried tomatoes**
- **Butter or oil**
- **Can or vacuum pack of tuna**
- **1/4 cup (50 g) Parmesan cheese**

30 min

2 pots

DIFFICULTY

Moderate

Make the crepes, set aside and keep warm.

In a skillet, sauté the garlic and the mushrooms. Blanch the tomatoes in a little boiling water for 2 minutes. Drain and finely chop. Add to the garlic and mushroom mixture. Set aside.

In a pot on a separate burner, prepare the cream sauce according to the directions on the package. Stir in the garlic, mushrooms, sun-dried tomatoes, the tuna and the Parmesan cheese.

Place a crepe on a plate. Spoon some of the mixture to one side and roll up. Serve two or three on each plate, depending on appetites. Sprinkle the top of each crepe with additional Parmesan cheese if desired.

This recipe can be readily adapted. Use your imagination and your favorite ingredients!

Serves 2

This recipe can serve four people with smaller appetites.

Variations:

scrambled eggs with bacon bits and onions, packaged Béarnaise sauce

canned chicken with sun-dried tomatoes, pesto cream sauce

chopped sausage, tomatoes, green pepper and shredded Cheddar

Crêpes with Pears and Two Cheeses

- Make the crêpe recipe from page 72
- 2 pears cut into thin slices
- 1/2 cup (100 g) blue cheese, crumbled
- 1/3 cup (60 g) Parmesan cheese
- 4 tablespoons (60 ml) butter

Cut the pears into thin slices. Place three or four slices on one half of a crêpe. Combine the two cheeses and sprinkle on top. Fold the crêpes in half and then in half again, forming a wedge.

Melt the butter in a skillet and sauté the crêpes on both sides until the crêpe is golden brown and the cheese is melted.

30 min

1 pot

DIFFICULTY

Easy

Serves 4

Variation:

Use apples instead of pears later in the trip.

The Sweet End of the Meal
DESSERTS

Unless you are carrying a collapsible oven, desserts in camp are usually simple, comprised of the fresh fruits brought along or, if you're lucky, some fresh berries gathered along the way, possibly accompanied by yogurt. Not that there's anything wrong with that; the vitamins and roughage provided by fruits are important. Fresh dates, dried fruit or commercially prepared puddings that need no refrigeration are welcome additions to the dessert menu. Often, just a cookie suffices with a cup of coffee when you're sitting around a campfire or watching the sun go down. By the end of the day, everyone is usually pretty tired and making dessert is not high on the priority list. Dishes have to be cleaned from the evening meal, food put away and stored or hung for the night. But you can prepare tasty treats if you have the time or inclination at the end of a meal.

Baked Apples with Raisins

This was one of the first recipes I prepared with a group of friends when I was in high school. Then, we wrapped the apples in pastry. I've modified the recipe to cook at camp, wrapping the apples instead in tin foil. This is a dessert to make on a late evening as the fire is dying. Assign one of the members of your group to prepare the apples before dinner so they are ready to cook.

If you have a leisurely day in camp, it can also be an inspired breakfast, served with granola or other hearty cereal.

- **4 whole apples**
- **1/4 cup (50 g) brown sugar**
- **1/4 cup (60 ml) butter**
- **1 teaspoon (5 g) cinnamon**
- **1/4 cup (50 g) raisins**

Core the apples. Mix together the other ingredients in a cup or small bowl. Stuff the centre of each apple with the sugar and butter mixture. Place each apple on a square of tin foil large enough to completely wrap it. Crinkle the top to seal the package. Place on a grill over a dying fire with good embers or a burner over low heat and cook for 20 or 30 minutes until the apple is cooked through.

30 min

1 pot

DIFFICULTY

Easy

Serves 4

Variation:

Add finely chopped walnuts to the mixture.

Spiced Apple Slices

- 1 apple, cored and cut into thick slices, crossways
- 2 tablespoons (30 ml) butter
- 1/2 teaspoon (2.5 g) cinnamon
- 1/4 teaspoon (1.25 g) nutmeg
- 2 tablespoons (20 g) brown sugar

At home, combine the spices and sugar and transport in a small plastic container if these ingredients aren't going to be used for other recipes chosen for the trip. Don't forget to label the container. Pack it with the apples.

Heat the butter in a skillet and sauté the apple slices for a minute or two. Turn over. Sprinkle half the spice mixture on top. Turn again. Sprinkle the remaining spice mixture on the second side of the apples.

Serve with aged Cheddar cheese or ginger snaps.

The apple slices can also be served as an accompaniment to dinner with ham or pork, or with bacon or sausages at breakfast.

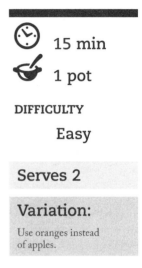

15 min

1 pot

DIFFICULTY

Easy

Serves 2

Variation:

Use oranges instead of apples.

Fried Bananas

At home, these bananas taste great served with a
dollop of ice cream. This is obviously not an option in
camp, but consider serving them with vanilla yogurt, early
in the trip, with unrefrigerated vanilla pudding or just on
their own.

- **2 bananas, sliced lengthwise**
- **1/4 cup (60 ml) butter**
- **1/4 cup (50 g) brown sugar**

Melt the butter in a skillet over low heat. Add the brown
sugar and combine until the sugar is melted. Take care
not to burn the mixture. Place the bananas, cut side down,
in the pan. Cook for a few minutes, until the bananas are
slightly browned. Turn over and cook for a few minutes
more. Drizzle the sauce over the bananas when serving.

🕐 **15 min**

🥄 **1 pot**

DIFFICULTY

Easy

Serves 4

- -

Fresh Fruit with Yogurt

- **fresh fruit you have brought
  or gathered along the way**
- **1 small container of yogurt**
- **toasted slivered almonds**
- **brown sugar**

This recipe is dead simple. Just combine any fruit you
have—sliced apples, orange segments, bananas, plums
or any other fruit on hand—with a container of yogurt. Stir
gently. Spoon into individual dishes, garnish with slivered
almonds and sprinkle with brown sugar.

🕐 **15 min**

DIFFICULTY

Easy

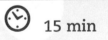

Serves 2

Dessert Crêpes

- **Crêpe batter recipe, page 72**
- **diced fruit—whatever you have on hand**
- **knob of butter**
- **1/2 teaspoon (2.5 g) cinnamon**
- **1/2 cup (100 g) chocolate chips**

Make the crêpes and cover to keep warm.

Melt the butter in a skillet and add the diced fruit. Sprinkle with cinnamon. Cook until the fruit is softened. Divide the fruit evenly between the crêpes, spreading it on one side of each crêpe. Sprinkle a few chocolate chips over the top of the fruit. Fold over the other side. Return the crêpes to the skillet. Cover and cook over low heat until the chocolate has melted, a minute or two. Drizzle with brandy or your favorite liqueur if you like.

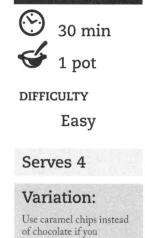

30 min

1 pot

DIFFICULTY

Easy

Serves 4

Variation:

Use caramel chips instead of chocolate if you have someone in your group who is allergic to chocolate.

Chocolate Fondue

- 1 cup (200 g) semi sweet chocolate chips
- 6 ounces (170 g) cream cheese
- 1/2 cup (120 ml) milk
- 3 tablespoons (45 ml) orange liqueur or brandy
- pieces of fruit such as melons, apples, bananas, pineapples, nectarines, oranges, kiwis, strawberries

In a small pot, over low heat, melt the chocolate chips, add the cream cheese, the milk and the liqueur. Stir until combined and smooth.

Using a fork, dip the fruit into the chocolate fondue and enjoy!

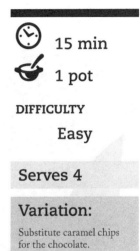

15 min

1 pot

DIFFICULTY

Easy

Serves 4

Variation:

Substitute caramel chips for the chocolate.

Mangoes in Cointreau

- 2 mangoes
- 1/4 cup (60 ml) Cointreau
- container of unrefrigerated vanilla pudding

After breakfast or lunch, peel and slice the mangoes and marinate them in the Cointreau in a sealed plastic container for an hour or so while in camp or paddling to your next camp.

Serve with a dollop of the vanilla pudding.

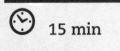

15 min

DIFFICULTY

Easy

Serves 4

Saucy Companions

SAUCES
& CONDIMENTS

A flavorful sauce can take a well-crafted meal to another level. It can also save a small disaster when something has been overcooked, or other culinary mishaps.

While camped on a small island in Harmony Islands Marine Park, I was preparing rotini with tuna, cherry tomatoes tossed with pesto sauce, pine nuts and Parmesan cheese. The rotini was bubbling along in the pot in front of me as I prepared the pesto sauce on another burner. I wanted to move the burner with the rotini and put my clamp on the lid of the pot. As I held the pot lid with one hand and tried to move the stove canister attached to the burner with the other, the pot overturned and the rotini spilled onto the ground in front of me. I gathered up the spilled pasta and rinsed it with some fresh water. The little bits of lichen were washed away. When I combined the pesto sauce and the other ingredients, my dinner was saved. No one was any the wiser!

Hunter's Sauce (Sauce Chausseur)

Apparently created by Duke Philippe De Mornay (1549–1623). He is also credited with creating Mornay Sauce, which bears his name, and Béchamel, Lyonnaise and Porto sauces. What a great paddling chef he would have been in camp!

Make at home, dry and then reconstitute at camp.

If you're on a short trip, freeze the sauce in a small, sealed container for transport. It goes well with beef or pork.

- 3/4 cup (150 g) finely chopped button mushrooms
- 2 green onions, finely chopped
- 1 tablespoon (10 g) flour
- 2 tablespoons (30 ml) butter
- 3/4 cup (175 ml) dry white wine
- 1 tablespoon (15 ml) tomato paste
- 1/4 cup (65 ml) beef broth
- salt and pepper
- 1/2 teaspoon (2.5 g) thyme
- 1 bay leaf
- 1/4 cup (50 g) finely chopped parsley or 2 teaspoons (10 g) freeze-dried parsley

Brown the mushrooms and chopped green onions in a skillet with butter. In a separate cup, stir the flour into the wine. Stir in the tomato paste. Add the spices. Add the liquid mixture to the skillet, and stir to combine. Simmer for five minutes or until thickened. Remove the bay leaf. Add the parsley and stir until incorporated into the sauce.

Cheese Sauce

- 2 tablespoons (30 ml) butter
- 2 tablespoons (30 g) flour
- 1 cup (250 ml) milk
- 1 tablespoon (15 ml) Dijon mustard
- 1/2 cup (125g) grated Parmesan, Cheddar or Asiago cheese
- pepper to taste

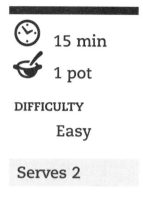

15 min

1 pot

DIFFICULTY

Easy

Serves 2

In a saucepan, melt the butter. Add the flour. Stir and cook for a few minutes to make a roux. Gradually add the milk, stirring until the sauce is thickened. Add the mustard and the cheese and stir until the cheese is melted. Season with pepper to taste. Add one-half teaspoon (2.5 g) crumbled dried herbs such as ore gano, thyme or basil for variation.

This versatile recipe can be spooned onto steamed vegetables such as broccoli or cauliflower, or on fresh-caught fish.

It can also be stirred into cooked pasta for an easy macaroni and cheese meal.

Top with bacon bits or serve with fried ham slices.

Homemade Mustard Sauce

Prepare this sauce at home and transport in a small container to use at the beginning of the trip with the fresh meat. It also works well with beef. Just combine the ingredients.

- 1/4 cup (60 ml) mayonnaise
- 2 tablespoons (30 ml) Dijon mustard
- 2 tablespoons (30 ml) yogurt
- dash of Tabasco or chili sauce
- freshly ground pepper
- 1 teaspoon (5 g) finely chopped chives or green onion

. . . .

Tzatziki

Tzatziki is a Greek dip and can accompany meat dishes. It is readily found in grocery stores but can be made at home and transported in a sealed plastic container. It will keep for three or four days. Here's a recipe if you want to make your own.

Variation:
Add 1 to 2 tbsp (15 to 30g) dill.

- 2 cups (500 ml) thick yogurt
- 5 to 10 cloves garlic, finely chopped
- 1/2 c (100 g) grated English cucumber
- 1 tbsp (15 ml) olive oil
- 2 tbsp (30 ml) lemon juice

Grate the cucumber over a small bowl. Squeeze out the moisture. Combine the cucumber with the remaining ingredients. Store in the fridge overnight before your trip, so the flavors will combine.

Pesto—a most versatile sauce

Pesto sauce originated in northern Italy and means 'pound or bruise' in Italian. It can be made from different combinations of ingredients, but is usually understood by North Americans as a green sauce comprised of basil, garlic, pine nuts and olive oil.

Concentrated pesto can be purchased in a tube that is easily transported on a paddling trip. Proportions are one teaspoon of concentrated pesto to a tablespoon of olive oil. It can also be combined with a little water from cooked pasta to make a smooth sauce tossed with Romano or Parmesan cheese.

Pesto can also be bought in a small jar from the website I've included in the bibliography, or from your local Italian or specialty market. In larger communities, pesto is readily available from your local grocer. Gourmet pestos include interesting combinations of flavors other than the one that I have described.

The uses for pesto are only limited by your culinary creativity. It can be added to a frittata, or tossed with ratatouille. Consider mixing with cream cheese to spread on rounds of a baguette and top with smoked salmon. Add pesto to a prepared package of Alfredo sauce for a creamy pesto Alfredo tossed with curly pasta.

Pesto is easily made at home and can be transported, frozen, in a plastic container, to enhance its longevity on a paddling trip.

PESTO
- **3 cloves garlic**
- **2 cups (400 g) fresh basil leaves**
- **1/2 cup (50 g) pine nuts**
- **dash of salt and pepper**
- **1/2 cup (125 ml) extra virgin olive oil**
- **1/2 cup (100 g) grated Parmesan cheese**

Make the pesto in either a blender or food processor. Mince the garlic. Add the garlic, basil leaves and pine nuts to your blender/processor and blend. Sprinkle the salt and pepper. With the blender/processor at a low speed, slowly drizzle in the olive oil. Remove the mix to a bowl and stir in the grated cheese until well combined.

Oil and Vinegar Dressing

Olive oil is best taken in a small jar or plastic bottle. Choose balsamic vinegar, white or red wine vinegar or just plain white vinegar, depending on your taste and the recipes you have chosen to make. Add a pinch of dried herbs for flavor to the vinegar. For salad dressing, the ratio for oil to vinegar is one part vinegar to four parts oil.

. . . .

Ghee

Ghee can be used in place of olive oil or fresh butter, and it's especially tasty with vegetables and potatoes. Similar to clarified butter, ghee will keep for 2 to 3 months at room temperature.

- **1 pound (.45 kg) unsalted butter, cut in quarters**

In a heavy saucepan, heat the butter over medium heat, melting it slowly. Do not let it brown. Increase the heat and bring to a boil until the surface is covered with a white foam. Immediately reduce the heat to its lowest point. Carefully skim off the foam with a spoon. Simmer uncovered and undisturbed for 45 minutes. Heating the butter in this manner evaporates its water content, producing a butter with a nutlike flavor. The milk solids on the bottom of the pot should be golden brown and the butter on the top should be clear.

Slowly pour the clear liquid ghee into a bowl, straining it through a fine sieve lined with several layers of dampened cheesecloth or a linen tea towel. When you are done, the ghee must be perfectly clear and have no solids. The ghee will go rancid otherwise. Repeat the straining process if necessary to ensure clarity. Pour into a jar or plastic bottle and cover tightly. Makes about 1½ cups (375 ml).

SAUCES FOR FISH

Traditional sauces; tartar, butter with lemon juice (with or without the addition of dill, parsley or capers), or teriyaki sauce are great to have on hand, but there are other interesting possibilities to enhance the flavor of your fresh-caught fish.

Anchovy Sauce

- 1 teaspoon (5 ml) anchovy paste
- 1 tablespoon (15 ml) butter
- 1 tablespoon (15 g) flour
- 1 cup (250 ml) milk (prepared from dried milk)
- salt, pepper

Melt the butter in a pot, add the flour and stir until combined, making a roux. Continue stirring on low heat for 2 to 3 minutes. Add the milk gradually, and simmer, stirring constantly, until the sauce thickens. Add the anchovy paste and salt and pepper. If the sauce is too thick, add a little water or white wine.

15 min

1 pot

DIFFICULTY

Easy

Variation:

Nap the fish with the sauce and garnish with a medium tomato, chopped.

Tomato Sauce with Garlic and Herbs

- 1/2 cup (125 ml) tomato sauce or the equivalent dried and reconstituted
- 3 tablespoons (45 ml) white wine
- 1 teaspoon (5 g) fresh basil, finely chopped or dried equivalent
- 1 teaspoon (5 g) fresh oregano, finely chopped or dried equivalent

Combine the ingredients together over low heat and simmer until heated through. Sauce your fresh-caught fish. Sprinkle with black olive slices, if desired. Garnish with a wedge of lemon.

This sauce can be prepared at home and dried in the same manner as other tomato based sauces.

15 min

1 pot

Vegetarian

DIFFICULTY

Easy

Burro Bianco

- 1/4 cup (60 ml) white wine vinegar
- 1/4 cup (60 ml) chicken bouillon
- 1 shallot, finely chopped
- 1/4 cup (50 ml) butter
- 1 teaspoon (5 g) dried tarragon

Melt the butter in a small pot. Add the shallot and cook until softened. Add the white wine vinegar and the bouillon. Whisk or stir until well blended and reduced. Add the tarragon. Remove from the heat and let sit for a few minutes for the flavors to meld.

This sauce is an excellent accompaniment for just about any fish.

15 min

1 pot

DIFFICULTY

Easy

The Hunter Gatherer

FORAGING
ALONG THE WAY

While eating well on a paddling trip means careful meal planning at home, finding fresh treats along the way can make meals even more special. Berries make a wonderful addition to pancakes, and can be sprinkled on top of cereal or incorporated into a salad or even a sauce.

Excellent varieties of mushrooms can be found in the forest, and edible greens such as goose tongue and sea asparagus are often prevalent near the shore. On a canoe/kayak trip on Sechelt Inlet with my daughter and our friends Martine and Rodney, we gathered sea asparagus on the shore when we stopped for a snack near the entrance to Narrows Inlet. Martine gathered the greens and we cooked the delicacy with a little butter, to accompany our evening meal. On our trip out of Kyuquot, Leslie found chanterelles while walking in the woods on Spring Island.

Catching fish can be a most satisfying part of a canoe or kayak trip. It requires time and effort, but if you have the opportunity to fish and are successful, you will be treated to a fresh meal unsurpassed by any other you pack (assuming that you're not a vegetarian). On Rodney's first raft trip on the Colorado River, the trout fishing was excellent, and he caught several one evening while others were preparing dinner. Unfortunately for him, the group consisted mostly of vegetarians and they were disgusted when he killed, cooked and ate the fat and delicious trout before their very eyes.

Berries

Many species of edible berries can be found on spring and summer paddling trips, and into early fall. Salmonberries, blackberries, salal berries, low bush cranberries and wild strawberries are happy finds. Most of these are not found near the seashore, but can be found nearby in open grassy or wooded areas. They are more readily found near lakes or rivers. One day, we found low bush cranberries near our camp on Isaac Lake; they made a tasty addition to the bannock we made that evening. With anything you find while foraging, never eat a berry if you are unsure of its identity. Like some species of mushrooms, certain berries are also poisonous.

Mushrooms

Mushroom picking is not permitted in many areas—national or provincial parks, ecological reserves and recreation areas—and requires permission on private land, First Nations reserve lands and leased public land. But should you find yourself in an area where gathering mushrooms can be an afternoon detective trip, you will think that you are Sherlock Holmes revisited should you be successful in finding these hidden gems.

Any wild mushroom picked should only be consumed in small quantities; not more than 150 grams for a species that you have never eaten, to preclude any adverse reaction. Some people are sensitive to species of mushrooms that others can eat heartily. Symptoms of mushroom poisoning can include headache, dizziness, diarrhea, blurred vision and gastrointestinal discomfort. Occasionally, death. Not to frighten the reader! Never eat a mushroom if you're unsure of its identity. When picking mushrooms in the wild, cut off the mushroom at ground level if you know that you are picking a chanterelle, Prince or other mushroom known to you. Mushrooms spread by mycelium under the ground and if the mushroom is pulled up, the mycelium can be destroyed and you won't have your cherished patch to visit the next time. Pat the soil back into place after removing the mushrooms. But if you're unsure, take the whole mushroom and have it properly identified when you get back home so that you will have more knowledge when embarking on your next adventure.

Chanterelles can be found all over Canada and the United States in temperate second growth forests of Douglas Fir and Hemlock and are easily identified, even by a novice mycologist. While not easy to find, they live in small patches, often in depressions filled with grass or leaf litter, or hide under bunches of salal. As immature mushrooms, they are small, gold buttons, but as they mature, they develop a golden, ruffled cap. Like all mushrooms, they favor moist conditions and are gathered from mid summer to late autumn, depending on the amount of rain that has fallen. They are firm in texture, don't shrink as much as commercial mushrooms do when cooked, and have a lovely, nutty flavor. The chanterelles that Leslie found on Spring Island greatly enhanced our dinner that evening. Sauté them in butter and sprinkle with a little salt. Add to omelettes, sauces or pasta dishes.

Other species quite easy to identify for the beginner, such as morels, prince, shaggy mane and boletus can also be found, depending on the location of your trip. I don't intend to delve into the specifics of mushroom gathering, but do consult reference materials, the Web and my bibliography on the subject.

Inland Greens

Wild Leeks

Wild leeks are found in sandy, moist habitat, near streams.
Their broad, smooth leaves are edible when tender in the spring.
The bulb is edible all year round. Tear off a leaf to identify the leek.
It has a characteristic onion smell. Prepare the leaves as you would
ordinary leeks, and treat the bulb as you would an onion.

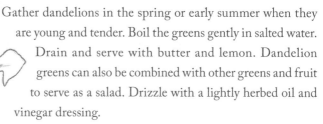

Dandelions

Gather dandelions in the spring or early summer when they
are young and tender. Boil the greens gently in salted water.
Drain and serve with butter and lemon. Dandelion
greens can also be combined with other greens and fruit
to serve as a salad. Drizzle with a lightly herbed oil and
vinegar dressing.

Fiddleheads

Fiddleheads are the young, coiled leaves of the ostrich fern and are gathered in the spring when the fern starts to leaf. They are identifiable in that they have papery, brown scales while most ferns have woolly fiddlehead sheaths. **CAUTION:** Be particularly careful that you do not confuse fiddleheads from the ostrich fern with those from the bracken fern, which are carcinogenic. The ostrich fern is found along streams and in damp areas, and grows in symmetrical, vase-shaped clumps. The bracken fern has fronds that are more branched: it colonizes in forest clearings and burnt areas.

Wash the fiddleheads, removing the brown scales. Cook in boiling water for 10 minutes or steam for 20 minutes. Toss with melted butter, lemon juice and tarragon.

Lamb's Quarters (Pigweed or Goosefoot)

The pale, bluish-green leaves of lamb's quarters are gathered in summer. Strip the upper leaves or pick the young plants when only a few inches high. Cook in a small amount of boiling water like you would spinach. Or, serve as a salad with herb dressing and crumbled feta cheese.

Greens Along The Shore

Sea Asparagus

Found growing just above the high tide line or in estuaries, this delicate vegetable looks like a petite version of its landlocked namesake. It is best from late May to July, but we gathered good quality greens at the entrance to Narrows Inlet in early August.

Blanch in boiling water for a few minutes. The sea asparagus should still have a nice crunch. Drain the hot water and toss with cold water to set the color. Drizzle with lemon, or lightly sauté with butter and garlic after blanching.

Goose Tongue

This traditional vegetable of the First Nations people is found above the high tide line. Gently boil the greens and toss with a little butter, salt and pepper.

Sea Lettuce

This light green 'lettuce' grows at the mid-tide mark. It, like most seaside greens, has a slightly salty flavor and can be mixed with other salad greens. Another possibility is to use it as a wrap to stuff with rice and dip in soy sauce, sushi style. Consider mixing other ingredients with the rice, such as finely chopped mushrooms, green onions or sun-dried tomatoes.

Dried in the sun and broken into crunchy pieces, it also makes a tasty pre-dinner snack.

No H20

DRYING FOOD FOR LONGER TRIPS

First Try at Drying Foods

Queen Charlotte Islands (Haida Gwaii) Gwaii Haanas Park
July 15 to August 2, 2002

Leslie and I have been planning our trip to Gwaii Haanas Park (Queen Charlotte Islands) for almost a year, in part because we enjoy the research and planning of our trips almost as much as the experience of paddling itself. The ancient rain forests and rugged beauty of this west coast archipelago, the rich, diverse marine ecosystem, the history of the Haida people and more recently of the European settlers, not to mention the significant paddling challenges, make Haida Gwaii the most exceptional region in British Columbia to explore.

We will begin our trip at Rose Harbour on the northern coast of Kunghit Island, facing the south coast of Moresby Island. This tiny, isolated community is home to three households: Patrich Lemaire and Mary Wright and their two young boys; across the bay, Susan Cohen and her neighbor, Gotz Hanisch. Rose Harbour is the location of a whaling station that existed from the 1800s until the early part of the twentieth century. Remains of boilers and other equipment are rusting away near Susan Cohen's home.

I also spent a great deal of time planning our meals for this trip. We would be on the water for two weeks, and making choices for good meals at the end of the trip was important. We wouldn't be able to take much fresh food, so I researched other possibilities. Many foods dry and reconstitute well, so I borrowed a food drier from my next door neighbor and enthusiastically dried mushrooms, beans and frozen mixed vegetables. These I stored in zip lock bags and kept in the fridge until our departure. Big mistake! I had not given the vegetables sufficient time to completely dry and the humidity in the fridge only compounded my problem. After we'd been out on the water for a week, paddling north up the east coast of Moresby Island in Gwaii Haanas Park, I turned to my dried food. All of the vegetables and mushrooms had gone moldy. This unfortunate outcome, combined with losing a dozen eggs when the branch broke as we were hauling our food up a big spruce at our camp on Isle

225, certainly put a damper on the more creative aspects of the cuisine I had planned for the latter part of the trip. My only success in drying, as it turned out, was the tomato sauce leather, which, when reconstituted, is just as tasty as the original.

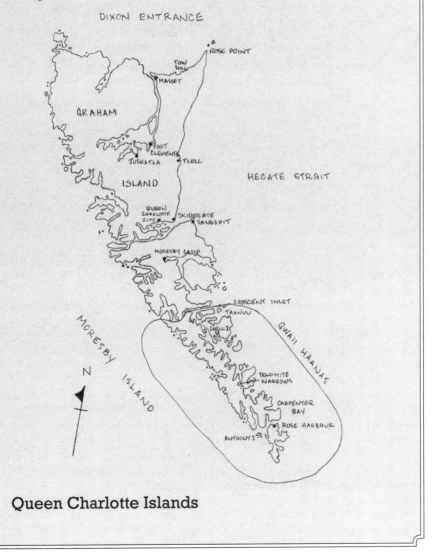

Queen Charlotte Islands

If properly dried, foods need to be sealed in airtight containers and do not need to be refrigerated. After all, that is the point! Be patient when drying food to ensure that you have extracted all the moisture.

Dried Tomato/Spaghetti Sauce

Line a cookie sheet with plastic wrap. Pour an eight-ounce can of tomato sauce, or spaghetti sauce onto the cookie sheet. Spread in a circle or rectangle, about one-quarter inch deep, a little thinner near the centre. Bake at the lowest temperature of the oven, 150°F. for approximately eight hours, leaving the oven door open a crack. Dry until the edges peel easily from the plastic and the centre is not sticky. Cool. Roll up in the plastic wrap while still malleable. Let the leather completely cool and store in an airtight container.

To use at camp, tear the dried sauce into small pieces and reconstitute with boiling water. Use approximately 4 parts water to 1 part dried sauce.

Other canned foods such as refried beans, chili and beef stew can also be successfully dried in the same manner. Cut up any larger pieces so that the food has an even texture. Be patient! Otherwise, you will discover that some pieces will dry more slowly than the rest and you will likely end up with moldy food.

Dried Vegetables

Precooked packages of frozen vegetables are the easiest to dry as they don't require blanching. Simply spread the vegetables on a drying rack in the oven at the lowest temperature and dry for eight hours or so, or use a commercial food dryer. Again, patience is a virtue when drying food. Make sure the vegetables are completely dry and cooled before sealing them in a zip lock bag.

If you want to dry fresh vegetables, they must be blanched before drying. Use only the best quality fresh vegetables, without cuts or bruises. They also must be in small, uniform pieces or they will dry unevenly and you will have a repeat of my Gwaii Haanas disaster.

Vegetables that will dry well include:
- Green beans
- Beans
- Corn niblets
- Zucchini slices
- Mixed vegetables
- Mushrooms

Dried Sausages

This is a time consuming process, but if you want meat at the end of a long trip—other than a tin of ham or canned chicken—it's worth the effort at home. Place precooked, skinless sausages on a pan lined with several layers of paper towels. Heat the oven to its lowest setting (150°F.) Dry for at least eighteen hours, replacing the paper towels as necessary as they absorb the fat from the sausages. They are done when the paper towels are fat free. These dehydrated sausages will keep for several weeks.

To reconstitute in camp, place the sausages in a skillet with a little water. Simmer and add more water, if necessary, until the sausages have plumped up to their original shape. Add a little butter or oil to the pan and fry the sausages for a minute or two to brown them.

Dried Hamburger and Other Meats

At home, cook lean hamburger or buffalo burger until brown. Break into small, even bits while cooking. Remove the cooked meat from the pan and place in a colander. Run under hot water until any remaining fat has been drained. Spread onto a baking sheet lined with paper towels and dry in the oven on low heat (150°F.) for several hours. As with the sausages, replace the paper towels as needed. Ground turkey, chicken, lamb or pork can also be dried in the same manner. The leaner the meat, the fewer paper towels will be needed. The absence of any fat on the towels will tell you that the meat is dried.

Reconstitute at camp, soaking the meat in water for 15 minutes. Approximately one-half cup (125 ml) of water will reconstitute 1 pound (.45 kg) of dried meat.

Dried Fruit

Fresh fruits can be dried at home to make fruit leather, just to be eaten at camp as a snack, or reconstituted to make apple or other sauces for use in recipes. Purée pieces of fresh fruit, or a combination that suits your taste, in a blender. Think of adding cinnamon or a splash of lemon juice to flavor. Pour the purée onto a plastic-lined cookie sheet, like the process for drying tomato sauce, and dry in the same manner. Wrap the fruit leather in the plastic wrap and store in an airtight container.

Other fruits, such as canned pineapple bits (drained), blueberries, thinly sliced apples, nectarines and peaches are easily dried to reconstitute at camp for use in favorite recipes. Frozen fruits dry well but as with vegetables, if you use fresh ones, select the best quality fruits at their peak of ripeness.

An easy option is to take already-dried fruits such as some of the ones mentioned, but also including apple or banana chips, dried apricots, prunes, cranberries and raisins. Your local bulk food store is an excellent source for dried fruits that can be purchased in small quantities.

Dried Tofu

The life of tofu can also be extended by dehydrating. Dehydrated, unseasoned tofu is available at Asian markets. But it can be dehydrated in the oven at home as well, using the same process as with meat. Cut a block of tofu into small squares, or crumble. Place onto a cookie sheet lined with a piece of paper towel. Firm tofu is the recommended variety; it will dry in a few hours. You can also sauté the tofu, adding flavors such as soy sauce, ginger or garlic and dry the cooked, flavored tofu.

Dried Herbs and Seasoning

Fresh herbs are easily taken on a short paddling trip but dried herbs can enhance meals on longer journeys. Dry them at home or just carry commercially prepared dried herbs. To dry herbs at home, place a paper towel in the microwave oven. Sprinkle a small handful of finely chopped, fresh herbs evenly over the paper towel. Set the microwave for 5 minutes on high. (The time may vary, depending on your own microwave oven.)

The ratio for fresh to dried is: 1 tablespoon (15 g) chopped, fresh herbs = 1 teaspoon (5 g) dried herbs.

Freeze-dried herbs can be found at some supermarkets and reconstitute even better than dried herbs when added to a sauce. The ratio for freeze-dried herbs to fresh is 1:1.

Chicken or beef bouillon can be taken either in cubes or as a powder to be used in sauces. The ratio for bouillon is: 1 cube to 1 cup (250 ml) hot water. Or use 1 rounded teaspoon of powdered bouillon to 1 cup (250 ml) water.

Powdered Milk

While most dairy products can be taken on a paddling trip; as I've already said, fresh milk is not one of them. But milk is a useful ingredient to have on hand to prepare cream sauces, baked goods—or simply to add to a cup of coffee or tea. If you'll be using more milk in the course of a day than in just one recipe, prepare a water bottle or thermos-sized container the night before. The milk will improve in flavor overnight.

The ratio for **dried milk** is one-quarter cup (60 ml) dried milk to 1 cup (250 ml) water.

Chocolate milk powder added to a mug of hot milk can warm and energize a weary paddler. Michael, Don and I landed to set up camp for our last night on the Bowron Lakes on a chilly, wet afternoon. Two men from Alberta, a father and son whose camp was already established nearby, graciously offered us a cup of hot chocolate or hot cider. This shared hospitality quickly rejuvenated us and brightened our spirits.

AFTERWORD

Some Culinary Musings

Breakfast, Lunch and Dinner

When the Sun Comes Up—Breakfast

The meal that should fuel us for the day is the one often neglected when we're wanting to get an early start on the water. There is nothing wrong with preparing a package of instant oatmeal with raisins, or eating a power bar when a six o'clock start is on the morning paddling agenda. However, a hearty breakfast, enjoyed when time isn't a consideration, can be a treasured part of the day as the rising sun warms the campsite.

- **Fresh or dried fruit** served with granola or other hearty cereals and a cup of hot chocolate provides an energy-fuelled start to the day. Of course, some of us need the kick of a good cup of coffee, too!
- **Yogurt** is an excellent, healthy complement to fruit or cereal.
- **Precooked bacon,** available at most grocery stores, is an easily prepared accompaniment to fried or poached eggs or, if time allows, pancakes.
- **Omelettes** can incorporate a wide variety of ingredients and provide a great opportunity to use up bits of leftover vegetables—mushrooms, onions, peppers and chopped tomatoes. Use your favourite herbs to add flavour: basil, oregano, dill. Grated cheese, added and melted as you turn the omelette, completes this top-of-the-line breakfast. Omelettes also make an easy lunch or dinner.

A Wet, Drippy Lunch

Bowron Lakes Provincial Park
September 5, 2003

The rain has let up in time for our departure in the morning, but increases in intensity as we cross Indianpoint Lake. A mucky landing on the east shore of the lake is miserable and the rain is continuous. The marsh is too shallow to allow paddling to the end of the lake, so two consecutive portages will have to be undertaken to access Isaac Lake. The awkward uphill portage on a rough, muddy trail is most unpleasant. We stop for lunch along the way and make hot green pea soup under the tenuous protection of a slender pine. My Tilley hat, given to me by Leslie last Christmas, is performing well in these wet conditions, as is the waterproof Helly Hansen jacket that Jim gave me. I'm disappointed that I have no cockpit cover for my kayak as the rain pours down.

The Easy Meal—Lunch

I have found lunches to be the easiest and most leisurely meal to prepare on paddling adventure. They are often eaten away from camp while exploring on a day trip. Breads, cheeses, deli meats, fruits and vegetables and soups can make up a satisfying lunch. Hard sausages such as pepperoni, Hunter sausage, salami and others will last for a week or more.

Dried or pre-packaged soups are also easy to prepare and feel especially satisfying on a wet or chilly day—as my Bowron Lake tale illustrates.

I have a fond memory of a simple lunch of pita bread, cheese, sausage and apples with a glass of cider enjoyed while spending a leisurely afternoon on a beautiful, sandy beach. We were on a tiny island in the Nuchatlitz area, off the west coast of Nootka Island.

Your own preferences and creativity are all you need to prepare tasty, enjoyable lunches. Look for ideas in the newspaper or magazines that you can adapt or simplify to take on a paddling adventure.

Dinner Reward at the
End of a Long Day
September 5, 2003

Finally, we have reached the west arm of Isaac Lake in Bowron Lakes
Provincial Park,and the opportunity to do some real paddling. We are
heading to Camp 15, just east of Wolverine Creek. This site has a cook
shelter and we're looking forward to this luxury and a chance to dry out.
I feel much better after establishing camp and changing into warm, dry
clothes, but now have two wet T-shirts and several damp items, including
my camp pillow, after only two days of paddling.

Dinner is on me this evening and I prepare fried ham with chanterelles
in Hunter's sauce and herbed mashed potatoes. Michael makes sautéed
cabbage with garlic to accompany. Altogether a hearty and tasty dinner.

Sharing this site is a young German couple whose dinner is a communal
bowl of pasta. They are surprised at the luxury of our meal—especially
when I pour my glass of white wine.

A young couple from Seattle who had arrived earlier, were packing up
when we put ashore, and left shortly after. They stayed only long enough
to dry out some gear and clearly had their own travelling agenda.

The rain has stopped but I'm not looking forward to donning my cold, wet
sprayskirt tomorrow morning. I haven't been this wet in all my years on
the water! We have a 25 kilometre paddle planned for tomorrow. This
will be good for me.

The End of the Day—Dinner

Dinner is usually the most anticipated meal on a paddling journey. Often, camp has been established earlier in the day and there is time to leisurely prepare a quality meal. Of course, this is not the case if weather and other circumstances get in the way.

So, some of the recipes I have included can be prepared in a short time if you have landed late in the day or are cooking under the tarp as the rain pours down. Others, you can enjoy on a sun drenched summer's evening. Use the recipes and adapt them to your own taste with additions or substitutions.

The Adventurous Chef

Canada and the United States are countries populated, with the exception of the First Nations people, of immigrants. For most of the history of our two countries these settlers have come from Europe. We have, over the years, incorporated French, Italian, Greek, Spanish and other culinary influences into our everyday meals. Some of the recipes in other sections of this book demonstrate these influences.

In the last thirty years or so, Vancouver, like other cities in Canada and the United States, has been transformed by virtue of immigrants coming from Korea, Hong Kong, China, Japan and India to establish a new home. The fortunate result of this multicultural influx has further expanded our tastes and our culinary horizons. Sushi is ubiquitous and Thai rice is not an unusual dish to accompany an everyday dinner. This just demonstrates to me how small the world has become and how food is the tie that binds us. I have included in this book some Thai, Indian, Chinese and Japanese recipes.

The paddling chef can easily incorporate some more exotic flavours into the menu. Many recipes are easy to prepare. You just need to make a little effort to seek out some special items from ethnic markets, and not rely solely on your nearby big chain grocery store for provisions. Go to your local bulk food store. You will find all sorts of interesting ingredients; specialty flours, rice, dried fruits and spices that can be bought in small amounts. Garlic and ginger pastes are available at Indian markets, as are specialty ingredients at Chinese, Japanese or Thai markets. If you live in a more remote community or small town where these are not options, search the Web. All sorts of specialty foods can be purchased online if you want to explore these possibilities. See my bibliography for a few suggestions.

Bibliography

Backlund, Gary and Grey, Paul. *Kayaking Vancouver Island: Great Trips from Port Hardy to Victoria,* Greyswan Publications, 2001.

Barber, James. *Peasant's Choice,* Urban Peasant Production Ltd., 1994.

Benoliel, Doug. *Northwest Foraging: Wild Edibles of the Pacific Northwest,* Signpost Book Publishing Company, 1974.

Challenger, Jean. *How to Cook Your Catch,* Saltaire Publishing Ltd., 1973.

Dominco, Terry. *Wild Harvest: Edible Plants of the Pacific Northwest,* Vancouver, B. C., Hancock House Publishers, 1979, 1982.

Fischer, David W., Alan E. Bessette. *Edible Wild Mushrooms of North America: A field to Kitchen Guide,* University of Texas Press, Austin, 1992.

Furlong, Marjorie. *Wild Edible Fruits and Berries,* Naturegraph, 1974.

Gabereau, Vicki. *Cooking Without Looking,* Douglas and McIntyre, 1994.

Gibbons, Euell. *Handbook of Edible Wild Plants,* Donning, 1979.

Gibbons, Euell. *Stalking the Wild Asparagus,* David McKay Co., 1971.

Glick, Judie and Fiona McLeod. *The Granville Island Market Cookbook,* Talonbooks, 1985.

Huser, Verne. *Paddle Routes of Western Washington—50 Flat Water Trips for Canoe and Kayak,* The Mountaineers Books, 2003.

Ince, John and Kottner, Heidi. *Sea Kayaking Canada's West Coast,* The Mountaineers Books, 1982.

Johnson, Eve and the Vancouver Sun Test Kitchen. *Six O'Clock Solutions,* Pacific Press Books, 1995.

Krumm, Bob, James Krumm. *The Pacific Northwest Berry Book,* Falcon Books, 1998.

McGee, Peter. *Kayak Routes of the Pacific Northwest Coast,* Greystone Books, 1998

McKenny, Margaret. *The Savory Wild Mushroom,* University of Washington Press, 1962; 1971.

McNair, James. *Cold Pasta,* Raincoast Books, Vancouver, B. C., Chronicle Books, San Francisco, California. 1985; 1989.

Menghi, Umberto. *The Umberto Menghi Cookbook,* Talonbooks, 1982.

Washburne, Randel and Gursten, Cary. *Kayaking Puget Sound, the San Juans and Gulf Islands: 50 trips on the Northwest's Inland Waters,* The Mountaineers Books, 2003.

Index

Websites

www.canoekayak.com:
Canoe & Kayak Magazine

www.paddlingcanada.com:
shows both canoe and kayak trips

www.paddling.net: canoe and kayak
multi-sport and fishing trips in
Canada and the United States

www.realadventures.com: canoeing
and kayaking in the United States

www.theforagerpress.com:
information about gathering wild
foods, especially mushrooms

www.wavelengthmagazine.com: a
free, comprehensive magazine
for paddlers

www.westerncanoekayak.com: a
large selection of book titles
for paddling B.C. and the
Pacific Northwest with books
on canoeing British Columbia
(including the Bowron Lakes
circuit), kayaking the B.C. west
coast and the Pacific Northwest

www.worldpantry.com: Annie
Chun's Shiitake Mushroom
Sauce and other packaged meals

More Great Books from Fox Chapel Publishing

Camp Cooking in the Wild
The Black Feather Guide to Eating Well in the Great Outdoors
By Mark Scriver, Joanna Baker, and Wendy Grater

Camp Cooking in the Wild can help you create a menu, set up a kitchen in the woods, and teach you new techniques and recipe ideas whether you are a beginner or a more experienced camper.

ISBN: 978-1-56523-715-5
$19.95 • 216 Pages

Recreational Kayaking
The Ultimate Guide
By Ken Whiting

This easy-to-read guide makes paddling fun and safe for both new and experienced paddlers looking to broaden their horizons.

ISBN: 978-1-56523-640-0
$19.95 • 192 Pages

Canoe Camping
An Essential Guide
By Mark Scriver

This comprehensive guide by senior guide and World Champion paddler Mark Scriver makes canoe camping fun and safe for both new and experienced canoe trippers.

ISBN: 978-1-56523-646-2
$16.95 • 112 Pages

Outdoor Parents Outdoor Kids
A Guide to Getting Your Kids Active in the Great Outdoors
By Eugene Buchanan

Award-winning author Eugene Buchanan extends parents a helping hand in getting their kids outside and instilling in them a respect for their health and the environment.

ISBN: 978-1-56523-635-6
$19.95 • 304 Pages